Merry Christmas 2003

To "Master Miller" From his satisfied customers Doug + Joan

D0899037

CONTENTS

~

The author and publishers
would like to thank the
following companies who lent
equipment and flours:
Prima International
Panasonic
PIFCO
Hinari
Pulse Home Products Ltd
West Mill Foods Ltd
Dove Farm Foods Ltd
Magimix

Introduction

In recent years there has been a huge upsurge in the popularity of home-baked bread. Men and women are coming home from work to the comforting aroma of freshly baked bread once only associated with an idyllic childhood. But making and eating home-baked bread is not only the stuff of dreams. No. The bread that stands cooling in many of our kitchens is real. It has a beautiful golden crust, an even crumb and a delicious flavour. It looks and tastes as if aching effort went into its making, but nothing could be further from the truth. Much of today's tastiest bread is made at home with the aid of an easy-to-operate machine, which takes the hard work out of bread making while retaining all the pleasure.

The first automatic domestic bread-maker appeared on the market in Japan in the late 1980s, and since then bread machines have gained popularity all over the world. These excellent appliances have helped to rekindle the pleasure of making home-made bread, by streamlining the process and making it incredibly simple. All the "home baker" needs to do is to measure a few ingredients accurately, put them into the bread machine pan and then push a button or two.

At first it is easy to feel overwhelmed by all the settings on a bread machine. These are there to help you bake a wide range of breads, both sweet and savoury, using different grains and flavourings. In time you'll get to grips with them all, but there's no need to rush. Start by making a simple white loaf and watch while your machine transforms a few ingredients first into a silky, smooth dough and finally into a golden loaf of bread.

No matter what make of machine you have, it is important to focus on the bread, not the machine. Even the best type of machine is only a kitchen aid. The machine will mix, knead and bake beautifully, but only after you have added the necessary ingredients and programmed it. The machine cannot think for itself; it can only carry out your instructions, so it is essential that you add the correct ingredients in the right proportions, in the order specified in the instructions for your particular bread-making machine, and that you choose the requisite settings. Do not become frustrated if your first attempts do not look one hundred per cent perfect; they will probably still taste wonderful. Get to know your bread machine and be willing to experiment to find the correct ratio of dry ingredients to liquids. There are a number of variables, including the type of ingredients used, the climate and the weather, which can affect the moisture level, regardless of the type of machine you are using.

When you make bread by hand you can feel whether it is too wet or dry, simply by kneading it. However, when you use a bread machine, you need to adopt a different strategy to determine if your bread has the right moistness and, if not, how you may adjust it to produce a perfect loaf.

After the machine has been mixing for a few minutes, take a quick look at the dough – it should be pliable and soft. When the machine stops kneading, the dough should start to relax back into the shape of the bread machine pan. Once you have made a few loaves of bread you will soon recognize what is an acceptable dough, and you will rapidly progress to making breads with different grains, such as rye, buckwheat or barley, or breads flavoured with vegetables. The range of both savoury and sweet breads you ultimately will be able to produce will only be limited by your imagination. Creative thinking can produce some magical results.

The breads in this book are either made entirely by machine or the dough is made in the machine, then shaped by hand and baked in a conventional oven. Teabreads are mixed by hand and baked in the bread machine. Where the loaves are made automatically you will usually find three separate lists of ingredients, each relating to a different size of machine. The small size is recommended for bread machines that are designed for loaves using 350–375g/12–13oz/3–3¼ cups of flour, the medium size for machines that make loaves using 450–500g/1lb–1lb 2oz/4–4½ cups of flour and the large size for bread machines that are capable of making loaves using up to 675g/1½lb/6 cups of flour. Refer to your manufacturer's handbook to check the capacity of your machine. If only one set of ingredients is given for a loaf that is to be baked automatically, relate these to the size of your machine to make sure it is suitable for the job. Where a bread machine is used solely for preparing the dough, which is then shaped by hand and baked conventionally, quantities are not so crucial, and only one set of ingredients is given.

It is very pleasurable to shape your own loaves of bread, and setting the machine to the "dough only" cycle takes all the hard work out of the initial mixing and kneading. The machine provides an ideal climate for the first rising period, leaving you to bring all your artistry to bear on transforming the dough into rolls, shaped breads or yeast cakes.

It is also possible to make gluten-free breads, but as this is a specialist area, it is best to follow the instructions given by your manufacturer, or contact their helpline, if you wish to do this.

INDEX

Bread making is a tremendously satisfying activity. With the help of your machine, delectable breads you will not find at the bakery or supermarket can be made with very little effort. From basic breads containing little more than flour, yeast and water to more elaborate loaves based on stoneground flours milled from a variety of grains – the possibilities are endless. What's more, you know precisely what goes into the bread, and can tailor loaves to your family's own tastes, adding sweet or savoury ingredients.

For everyday use, basic white loaves, possibly enriched with milk or egg, or flavoursome Granary and Light Wholemeal Breads are perfect for breakfast, whether freshly baked or toasted, and these can also be used for sandwiches and quick snacks. These types of bread are the easiest to make in your machine and are the ones you are likely to make over and over again. In time, however, you will probably progress to baking loaves with added ingredients such as potato, to provide, for example, an enhanced lightness to the dough. Leftover rice makes a tasty bread; and another delicious treat is the New England Anadama Bread, made from a blend of white, wholemeal and maizemeal (cornmeal) flours flavoured with molasses.

ABOVE: Hazelnut Twist Cake

With the addition of other grains, you can make more complex, hearty loaves. Breads containing oats, rye, wheatgerm and wild rice, perhaps with added whole seeds and grains, can all be baked in the bread machine. These provide extra fibre and are a good source of complex carbohydrates, and are thus a wonderfully healthy option as well as being simply scrumptious. Try Multigrain Bread, a flavour-packed healthy loaf made from Granary, rye and wholemeal flours with whole oats. Alternatively, experiment with a mixed-seed bread such as Four Seed Bread. The added seeds not only contribute crunchiness and flavour, but are also very nutritious.

The bread machine will happily incorporate such ingredients as caramelized onions, sun-dried tomatoes, char-grilled peppers, crispy bacon, slivers of ham and other cured meats, fresh chopped herbs and grated or crumbled cheese, to produce mouthwatering vegetable and other savoury breads. Spices and nuts, and dried, semi-dried and fresh fruits can also be added to make classic malted fruit loaves. Try succulent Cranberry and Orange Bread or Hazelnut and Fig Bread. Other sweet breads include crunchy Buckwheat and Walnut Bread and – every chocolate lover's dream – Three Chocolate Bread.

You can also cook succulent teabreads, Honey Cake, Gingerbread, Madeira Cake and Coconut Cake, to name but a few,

BELOW: Strawberry Teabread

BANANA AND PECAN TEABREAD

This moist, light teabread is flavoured with banana, lightly spiced with nutmeg and studded with sultanas and pecan nuts. Weigh the bananas after peeling them – it is important to use the precise quantities given.

SMALL

75g/3oz/6 tbsp butter, softened
150g/5½oz/generous ¾ cup caster (superfine) sugar
2 eggs, lightly beaten
175g/6oz/1½ cups self-raising (self-rising) flour, sifted
150g/5½oz peeled ripe bananas
70ml/2½fl oz/5 tbsp buttermilk
1.5ml/¼ tsp baking powder
2.5ml/½ tsp freshly grated nutmeg
100g/3½oz/generous ½ cup sultanas (golden raisins)
65g/2½oz/generous ½ cup pecan nuts, chopped
15ml/1 tbsp banana or apricot jam, melted
15ml/1 tbsp banana chips

MEDIUM

100g/3½oz/7 tbsp butter, softened
175g/6oz/⅞ cup caster sugar
2 large eggs, lightly beaten
200g/7oz/1¾ cups self-raising flour, sifted
200g/7oz peeled ripe bananas
85ml/3fl oz/6 tbsp buttermilk
2.5ml/½ tsp baking powder
5ml/1 tsp freshly grated nutmeg
125g/4½oz/⅔ cup sultanas
75g/3oz/¾ cup pecan nuts, chopped
30ml/2 tbsp banana or apricot jam, melted
30ml/2 tbsp banana chips

LARGE

115g/4oz/½ cup butter, softened
200g/7oz/1 cup caster sugar
3 eggs, lightly beaten
225g/8oz/2 cups self-raising flour, sifted
225g/8oz peeled ripe bananas
100ml/3½fl oz/7 tbsp buttermilk
2.5ml/½ tsp baking powder
5ml/1 tsp freshly grated nutmeg
140g/5oz/scant 1 cup sultanas
90g/3½oz/scant 1 cup pecan nuts, chopped
30ml/2 tbsp banana or apricot jam, melted
30ml/2 tbsp banana chips

MAKES 1 TEABREAD

1 Remove the kneading blade from the bread pan and line the base of the pan with baking parchment or greased greaseproof (waxed) paper.

2 Cream the butter and caster sugar in a mixing bowl until pale and fluffy. Gradually beat in the eggs, beating well after each addition, and adding a little of the flour if the mixture starts to curdle.

3 Mash the bananas until completely smooth. Beat into the creamed mixture with the buttermilk.

4 Sift the remaining flour and the baking powder into the bowl. Add the nutmeg, sultanas and pecans; beat until smooth.

5 Spoon into the prepared bread pan. Set the machine to the "bake only" setting. Set the timer, if possible, for the recommended time. If not, set the timer and check the cake after the shortest recommended time. Bake the small or medium cake for 55–60 minutes and the large cake for 65–70 minutes. Test by inserting a skewer in the centre of the teabread. It should come out clean. If necessary, bake for a few minutes more.

6 Remove the pan from the machine. Leave it to stand for about 5 minutes, then turn the cake out on to a wire rack.

7 While the cake is still warm, brush the top with the melted jam and sprinkle over the banana chips. Leave to cool completely before serving.

which provides an alternative to using your traditional oven for one cake. Fresh fruits such as strawberries and raspberries plus more exotic offerings can also be used as flavourings for these tea-time treats, as can traditional dried fruits, such as apricots, dates, prunes, sultanas and raisins.

These breads, mixed, proved and baked automatically, illustrate just a part of the bread machine's capabilities. You

BELOW: A flavoured bread, such as Grainy Mustard and Beer Loaf, is delicious served with cheese and pickle as a simple lunch.

can also use the "dough only" setting to make an endless variety of doughs for hand-shaping. Classic French breads, such as Fougasse, Couronne, croissants and baguettes, or rustic breads, such as Pain de Campagne and Russian Black Bread are all possible, as are Italian breads, such as Ciabatta, Pane all'Olio and Breadsticks (grissini). You will be able to experiment in making flatbreads such as Indian Naan, Italian Focaccia, Carta di Musica, Sfincione or pizzas.

Sweet yeast doughs also work well in a bread machine. Try making Strawberry Chocolate Savarin, Peach Brandy Babas

or Hazelnut Twist Cake, as well as strudels and classic festive breads such as Polish Babka (Easter bread) or British Hot Cross Buns. You can even impress your friends by baking a traditional Spiced Fruit Kugelhopf.

There are endless shaped rolls, buns and pastries to try out, from savoury Mixed Grain Onion Rolls to Parker House Rolls from Boston, and traditional Yorkshire Teacakes. All these breads can be easily shaped by hand after the machine has mixed and proved the dough, and then baked to golden perfection in a conventional oven.

STRAWBERRY TEABREAD

Perfect for a summertime treat, this hazelnut-flavoured teabread is laced with luscious fresh strawberries.

SMALL
115g/4oz/1 cup strawberries
115g/4oz/½ cup butter, softened
115g/4oz/generous ½ cup caster (superfine) sugar
2 eggs, beaten
140g/5oz/1¼ cups self-raising (self-rising) flour, sifted
25g/1oz/¼ cup ground hazelnuts

MEDIUM
170g/6oz/1½ cups strawberries
140g/5oz/⅔ cup butter, softened
140g/5oz/¾ cup caster sugar
2 eggs, beaten
15ml/1 tbsp milk
155g/5½oz/1⅓ cups self-raising flour, sifted
40g/1½oz/⅓ cup ground hazelnuts

LARGE
200g/7oz/1¾ cups strawberries
175g/6oz/¾ cup butter, softened
175g/6oz/⅞ cup caster sugar
3 eggs, beaten
175g/6oz/1½ cups self-raising flour, sifted
50g/2oz/½ cup ground hazelnuts

MAKES 1 TEABREAD

1 Remove the kneading blade from the bread pan and line the base of the pan with baking parchment or greased greaseproof (waxed) paper.

2 Hull the strawberries and chop them roughly. Set them aside. Cream the butter and sugar in a mixing bowl until pale and fluffy.

3 Gradually beat in the eggs and milk (if you are making the medium cake), beating well after each addition to combine quickly without curdling.

4 Mix the self-raising flour and the ground hazelnuts together and gradually fold into the creamed mixture, using a metal spoon.

5 Fold in the strawberries and spoon the mixture into the prepared bread pan. Set the machine to the "bake only" setting. Set the timer, if possible, for the recommended time. If, on your bread machine, the minimum time on the "bake only" setting is longer than the time suggested here, set the timer and check after the shortest recommended time. Bake the small or medium teabread for 45–50 minutes and the large teabread for 55–60 minutes.

6 Test by inserting a skewer in the centre of the teabread. It should come out clean. If necessary, bake for a few minutes more.

7 Remove the bread pan. Leave the teabread to stand for 2–3 minutes, then turn out on to a wire rack to cool.

A bread machine is designed to take the hard work out of making bread. Like most kitchen appliances, it is a labour-saving device. It will mix the ingredients and knead the dough for you, and allows the bread to rise and bake at the correct time and temperature.

For most breads, all you will need to do is to measure the ingredients for your chosen bread, put them into the pan in the correct order, close the lid, select a suitable baking programme and opt for light, medium or dark crust. You may also choose to delay the starting time, so that you have freshly baked bread for breakfast or when you return from work. Press the Start button and in a few hours you will have a beautifully baked loaf, the machine having performed the kneading, rising and baking cycles for you.

Bread machines offer a selection of programmes to suit different types of flour and varying levels of sugar and fat. You can explore making a whole variety of raw

BELOW. The three different sizes of bread machine pans that are available. From left to right: large, small and medium.

ABOVE: The shape of the kneading blade varies among different models of bread machine.

doughs for shaping sweet and savoury breads, sourdough breads, mixed-grains, Continental-style breads and many more.

All bread machines work on the same basic principle. Each contains a removable non-stick bread pan, with a handle, into which a kneading blade is fitted. When inserted in the machine, the pan fits on to a central shaft, which rotates the blade. A lid closes over the bread pan so that the ingredients are contained within a controlled environment. The lid includes an air vent and may have a window, which can be useful for checking the progress of your bread. The machine is programmed by using the control panel.

The size and shape of the bread is determined by the shape of the bread pan. There are two shapes currently available; one rectangular and the other square. The rectangular pan produces the more traditional shape, the actual size varying from one manufacturer to another. The square shape is mostly to be found in smaller machines and produces a tall loaf, which is similar to a traditional rectangular loaf that has been stood on its end. The vertical square loaf can be turned on its side for slicing, if preferred, in order to give smaller slices of bread.

The size of the loaf ranges from about 500g/1lb 2oz to 1.4kg/3lb, depending on the machine, with most large machines offering the option of baking smaller loaves as well. One machine will make small, medium and large loaves.

BUYING A BREAD MACHINE
There is plenty of choice when it comes to selecting a bread machine to buy. Give some thought to which features would prove most useful to you, then shop around for the best buy available in your

TREACLE, DATE AND WALNUT CAKE

Layered with date purée and finished with a crunchy sugar and walnut topping, this cake is absolutely irresistible.

SMALL
115g/4oz/⅔ cup pitted dates
grated rind and juice of ½ lemon
115g/4oz/1 cup self-raising
(self-rising) flour
2.5ml/½ tsp each ground cinnamon,
ginger and grated nutmeg
50g/2oz/¼ cup butter
50g/2oz/¼ cup light muscovado
(brown) sugar
15ml/1 tbsp treacle (molasses)
30ml/2 tbsp golden (light corn) syrup
40ml/2½ tbsp milk
1 egg
40g/1½oz/⅓ cup chopped walnuts

MEDIUM
140g/5oz/scant 1 cup pitted dates
grated rind and juice of 1 lemon
170g/6oz/1½ cups self-raising flour
3.5ml/¾ tsp each ground cinnamon,
ginger and grated nutmeg
75g/3oz/6 tbsp butter
75g/3oz/6 tbsp light muscovado sugar
22ml/1½ tbsp treacle
45ml/3 tbsp golden syrup
60ml/4 tbsp milk
1 large egg
50g/2oz/½ cup chopped walnuts

LARGE
170g/6oz/1 cup pitted dates
grated rind and juice of 1 lemon
225g/8oz/2 cups self-raising flour
5ml/1 tsp each ground cinnamon,
ginger and grated nutmeg
115g/4oz/½ cup butter
115g/4oz/½ cup light muscovado sugar
30ml/2 tbsp treacle
60ml/4 tbsp golden syrup
80ml/3fl oz/⅓ cup milk
1 large egg
75g/3oz/¾ cup chopped walnuts

TOPPING FOR ALL SIZES OF LOAF
25g/1oz/2 tbsp butter
50g/2oz/¼ cup light muscovado sugar
22ml/1½ tbsp plain (all-purpose) flour
3.5ml/¾ tsp ground cinnamon
40g/1½oz/⅓ cup chopped walnuts

MAKES 1 CAKE

1 Remove the kneading blade from the bread pan and line the base with baking parchment or greased greaseproof (waxed) paper. Mix the dates, lemon rind and lemon juice in a pan. Add 60ml/4 tbsp of water and bring to the boil, then simmer until soft. Purée in a blender or food processor until smooth.

2 Sift the flour and spices together. Cream the butter and sugar until pale and fluffy. Warm the treacle, golden syrup and milk in a pan, until just melted then beat into the creamed butter mixture. Add the egg and beat in the flour mixture. Stir in the walnuts.

COOK'S TIP
Try increasing the quantities of the toppings by 25 per cent if you are making a large cake, or decrease by 25 per cent if you are making a small cake.

3 Place half the mixture in the bread pan. Spread over the date purée, leaving a narrow border of cake mix all round. Top with the remaining cake mixture, spreading it evenly over the date purée.

4 Set the machine to the "bake only" setting. Set the timer, if possible, for the recommended time. If not, set the timer and check after the recommended time. Bake the small cake for 35 minutes, the medium cake for 40 minutes and the large cake for 45 minutes.

5 Mix all of the topping ingredients together. When the cake has baked for the recommended time, sprinkle the topping over and cook for 10–15 minutes more, until the topping starts to bubble and the cake is cooked. Remove the bread pan from the machine. Leave to stand for 10 minutes, then turn out on to a wire rack to cool.

price range. First of all, consider the size of loaf you would like to bake. Remember that a large bread machine will often make smaller loaves but not vice versa.

You will need to consider whether the shape of the bread is important to you, and choose a machine with a square or rectangular bread pan accordingly.

Think about what you want to make with your machine. Do you want to make breads with added ingredients? If so, a raisin beep is useful. Does the bread machine have speciality flour cycles for whole wheat loaves? Another feature, the dough cycle, adds a great deal of flexibility, as it allows you to make hand-shaped breads. Extra features, such as jam-making and rice-cooking facilities, are very specialized and only you can know whether you would find them worth having.

One important consideration is whether the manufacturer offers a well-written manual and an after-sales support system

or help line. If these are available, any problems or queries you might have can be answered quickly, which is particularly useful if this is your first machine.

A bread machine takes up a fair amount of room, so think about where you will store it, and buy one that fits the available space. If the bread machine is to be left on the work surface and aesthetics are important to you, you'll need to buy a machine that will be in keeping with your existing appliances. Most bread machines are available in white or black, or in stainless steel.

Jot down the features important to you, listing them in order of your preference. Use a simple

process of elimination to narrow your choice down to two or three machines, which will make the decision easier.

BELOW: A typical bread machine. Although each machine will have a control panel with a different layout, most of the basic features are similar. More specialist cycles vary from machine to machine.

BUILT-IN SAFETY DEVICES

Most machines include a power failure override mode which can prove to be extremely useful. If the machine is inadvertently unplugged or there is a brief power cut the programme will continue as soon as the power is restored. The maximum time allowed for loss of power varies from 10 to 30 minutes. Check the bread when the power comes back on; depending on what stage the programme had reached at the time of the power cut, the rising or baking time of the loaf may have been affected.

An over-load protection is fitted to some models. This will cut in if the kneading blade is restricted by hard dough and will stop the motor to protect it. It will automatically re-start after about 30 minutes, but it is important to rectify the problem dough first. Either start again or cut the dough into small pieces and return it to the bread pan with a little more liquid to soften the dough.

PEANUT BUTTER TEABREAD

Peanut butter is used instead of butter or margarine in this tasty teabread, giving it a distinctive flavour and an interesting texture, thanks to the peanut pieces.

SMALL
75g/3oz/¼ cup crunchy peanut butter
65g/2½oz/⅓ cup caster
(superfine) sugar
1 egg, lightly beaten
105ml/7 tbsp milk
200g/7oz/1¾ cups self-raising
(self-rising) flour

MEDIUM
115g/4oz/⅛ cup crunchy
peanut butter
75g/3oz/scant ½ cup caster sugar
1 egg, lightly beaten
175ml/6fl oz/¾ cup milk
300g/10½oz/generous 2½ cups self-
raising flour

LARGE
150g/5½oz/scant ½ cup crunchy
peanut butter
125g/4½oz/scant ¾ cup caster sugar
2 eggs, lightly beaten
200ml/7fl oz/⅞ cup milk
400g/14oz/3½ cups self-raising flour

MAKES 1 TEABREAD

1 Remove the kneading blade from the bread pan and line the base of the pan with baking parchment or greased greaseproof (waxed) paper.

2 Cream the peanut butter and sugar in a bowl together until light and fluffy, then gradually beat in the egg(s).

3 Add the milk and flour and mix with a wooden spoon.

COOK'S TIP
Leave a rough finish on the top of the cake before baking to add character.

4 Spoon the mixture into the prepared bread pan and set the machine to the "bake only" setting.

5 Set the timer for the recommended time. If the minimum time on the "bake only" setting on your machine is longer than the time suggested here, then set the timer and check the teabread after the shortest recommended time. Bake the small or medium teabread for 45–50 minutes, and the large teabread for 60–65 minutes.

6 The teabread should be well risen and just firm to the touch. Test by inserting a skewer in the centre of the teabread. It should come out clean. If necessary, bake for a few minutes more.

7 Remove the bread pan from the bread machine. Leave it to stand in the pan for 2–3 minutes, then transfer on to a wire rack to cool.

HOW TO USE YOUR BREAD MACHINE

The instructions that follow will help you to achieve a perfect loaf the first time you use your bread machine. The guidelines are general, that is they are applicable to any bread machine, and should be read in conjunction with the handbook provided for your specific machine. Make sure you use fresh, top quality ingredients; you can't expect good results with out-of-date flour or yeast.

1 Stand the bread machine on a firm, level, heat-resistant surface. Place away from any heat source, such as a cooker or direct sunlight, and also in a draught-free area, as these factors can affect the temperature inside the machine. Do not plug the bread machine into the power socket at this stage. Open the lid. Remove the bread pan by holding both sides of the handle and pulling upwards or twisting slightly, depending on the design of your particular model.

2 Make sure the kneading blade and shaft are free of any breadcrumbs left behind when the machine was last used. Fit the kneading blade on the shaft in the base of the bread pan. The blade will only fit in one position, as the hole in the blade and the outside of the shaft are D-shaped.

3 Pour the water, milk and/or other liquids into the bread pan, unless the instructions for your particular machine require you to add the dry ingredients first. If so, reverse the order in which you add the liquid and dry ingredients, putting the yeast in the bread pan first.

4 Sprinkle over the flour, ensuring that it covers the liquid completely. Add any other dry ingredients specified in the recipe, such as dried milk powder. Add the salt, sugar or honey and butter or oil, placing them in separate corners so they do not come into contact with each other.

SPECIAL FEATURES

Extra programmes can be found on more expensive machines. These include cooking jam or rice and making pasta dough. While these facilities would not be the main reason for buying a bread machine they can be useful extras. For instance, jam-making couldn't be easier: you simply add equal quantities of fresh fruit and sugar to the bread machine pan, set the jam programme and, when the cycle ends, you will have jam ready to pour into clean sterilized jars.

EASY MEASURING

If you have a set of electronic scales with an add and weigh facility, then accurate measuring of ingredients is very easy. Stand the bread pan on the scale, pour in the liquid, then set the display to zero. Add the dry ingredients directly to the pan, each time zeroing the display. Finally, add the fat, salt, sweetener and yeast and place the bread pan in your machine.

5 Make a small indent in the centre of the flour (but not down as far as the liquid) with the tip of your finger and add the yeast. If your indent reached the liquid below the dry ingredients, then the yeast would become wet and would be activated too quickly. Wipe away any spillages from the outside of the bread pan.

6 Place the pan inside the machine, fitting it firmly in place. Depending on the model of your machine, the pan may have a designated front and back, or clips on the outer edge which need to engage in the machine to hold the bread pan in position. Fold the handle down and close the lid. Plug into the socket and switch on the power.

AMERICAN COFFEE BREAD

This quick and easy sweet bread keeps well and so makes a useful standby.

SMALL

*175g/6oz/1½ cups plain
(all-purpose) flour
7.5ml/1½ tsp baking powder
pinch of salt
75g/3oz/6 tbsp light muscovado
(brown) sugar
50g/2oz/½ cup pecan nuts, chopped
7.5ml/1½ tsp instant coffee
20g/¾oz/1½ tbsp butter, melted
75ml/5 tbsp milk
1 egg, lightly beaten*

MEDIUM

*200g/7oz/1¾ cups plain flour
10ml/2 tsp baking powder
pinch of salt
100g/3½oz/scant ½ cup light
muscovado sugar
75g/3oz/¾ cup pecan nuts, chopped
10ml/2 tsp instant coffee
25g/1oz/2 tbsp butter, melted
100ml/3½fl oz/7 tbsp milk
2 eggs, lightly beaten*

LARGE

*280g/10oz/2½ cups plain flour
15ml/1 tbsp baking powder
pinch of salt
150g/5½oz/⅔ cup light muscovado sugar
115g/4oz/1 cup pecan nuts, chopped
15ml/1 tbsp instant coffee
40g/1½oz/3 tbsp butter, melted
160ml/5½fl oz/⅔ cup milk
2 eggs, lightly beaten*

MAKES 1 LOAF

COOK'S TIP
For a special tea-time treat, drizzle
the loaf with coffee glacé icing and
decorate with pecan nut halves.

1 Remove the kneading blade from the
bread pan and line the base of the pan
with baking parchment or greased
greaseproof (waxed) paper.

2 Sift the flour, baking powder and salt into
a large bowl. Stir in the sugar and pecan
nuts. Dissolve the coffee granules or powder
with 15ml/1 tbsp hot water in a cup.

3 Add the coffee, the melted butter,
milk and egg(s), to the dry ingredients.
Beat thoroughly to mix. Spoon the
mixture into the prepared bread pan
and set the bread machine to the "bake
only" setting.

4 Set the timer, if possible, for the
recommended time. If not, set
the timer and check after the shortest
recommended time. Bake the small
cake for 40–45 minutes, the medium
for 45–50 minutes and the large for
55–60 minutes.

5 Test by inserting a skewer into the centre
of the loaf. It should come out clean. If
necessary, bake for a few minutes more.

6 Remove the bread pan from the
machine. Let stand for 2–3 minutes,
then turn the bread out on to a wire
rack to cool.

7 Select the programme you require, including crust colour and loaf size, if available. Press Start. The kneading process will begin, unless your machine has a "rest" period to settle the temperature first.

8 Towards the end of the kneading process the machine will beep to alert you to add any additional ingredients, such as dried fruit, if wished. Open the lid, add the extra ingredients, and close the lid again.

9 At the end of the cycle, the machine will beep once more to let you know that the dough is ready or the bread is cooked. Press Stop. Open the lid of the machine. If you are removing baked bread, remember to use oven gloves to lift out the bread pan, as it will be extremely hot. Avoid leaning over and looking into the machine when you open the lid as the hot air escaping from the machine could cause you discomfort.

BELOW: A basic white bread is an excellent choice for the novice bread maker. If you follow these instructions and weigh the ingredients carefully, you are sure to achieve a delicious loaf of bread. Once you have gained confidence, experiment with the recipe, by adding other ingredients or changing the crust colour.

10 Still using oven gloves, turn the pan upside down and shake it several times to release the bread. If necessary, tap the base of the pan on a heatproof board.

11 If the kneading blade for your bread machine is not of the fixed type, and comes out inside the bread, use a heat-resistant utensil to remove it, such as a wooden spatula. It will come out easily.

12 Place the bread on a wire rack to cool. Unplug the bread machine and leave to cool before using it again. A machine which is too hot will not make a successful loaf, and many will not operate if they are too hot for this reason. Refer to the manufacturer's manual for guidance. Wash the pan and kneading blade and wipe down the machine. All parts of the machine must be cool and dry before you store it.

How to Use Your Bread Machine

Vanilla-chocolate Marble Cake

White and dark chocolate, marbled together, make a cake that tastes as good as it looks. Serve it for tea, or cut it into chunks, mix it with fresh peach slices and add a sprinkling of orange or peach liqueur for an impressive dessert.

1 Remove the blade from the bread pan and line the base with baking parchment or greased greaseproof (waxed) paper. Cream the margarine or butter and sugar together until light and fluffy. Slowly add the eggs, beating thoroughly. Place half the mixture in another bowl.

2 Place the white chocolate in a heatproof bowl over a pan of simmering water. Stir until the chocolate is melted.

3 Melt the plain chocolate in a separate bowl, in the same way. Stir the white chocolate and the vanilla essence into one bowl of creamed mixture and the plain chocolate into the other. Divide the flour equally between the two bowls and lightly fold it in with a metal spoon.

4 Put alternate spoonfuls of the two mixtures into the prepared bread pan. Use a round-bladed knife to swirl the mixtures together to marble them.

5 Set the bread machine to the "bake only" setting. Set the timer, if possible, for the recommended time. If not, set the timer and check the cake after the shortest recommended time. Bake the small cake for 45–50 minutes, the medium for 50–55 minutes and the large for 65–70 minutes, until well risen.

SMALL
115g/4oz/½ cup margarine or butter
115g/4oz/generous ½ cup caster (superfine) sugar
2 eggs, lightly beaten
40g/1½oz white chocolate, in pieces
40g/1½oz plain (semisweet) chocolate, in pieces
1.5ml/¼ tsp vanilla essence (extract)
175g/6oz/1½ cups self-raising (self-rising) flour
icing (confectioners') sugar and cocoa powder (unsweetened), for dusting

MEDIUM
125g/4½oz/generous ½ cup margarine or butter
125g/4½oz/scant ¾ cup caster sugar
2 eggs, lightly beaten
50g/2oz white chocolate, in pieces
50g/2oz plain chocolate, in pieces
2.5ml/½ tsp vanilla essence
200g/7oz/1¾ cups self-raising flour
icing sugar and cocoa powder, for dusting

LARGE
200g/7oz/scant 1 cup margarine or butter
200g/7oz/1 cup caster sugar
3 eggs, lightly beaten
75g/3oz white chocolate, in pieces
75g/3oz plain chocolate, in pieces
2.5ml/½ tsp vanilla essence (extract)
280g/10oz/2½ cups self-raising flour
icing sugar and cocoa powder, for dusting

MAKES 1 CAKE

6 The cake should be just firm to the touch. Test by inserting a skewer into the centre of the cake. It should come out clean. If necessary, bake for a few minutes more. Remove the pan from the machine. Stand for 2–3 minutes, then turn the cake out on to a wire rack. Dust with icing sugar and cocoa powder and serve in slices or chunks.

BASIC CONTROLS

It will take you a little while and some practice to become familiar with and confident about using your new bread machine. Most manufacturers now produce excellent manuals, which are supplied with their machines. The manual is a good place to start, and should also be able to help you if you come up against a problem. Programmes obviously differ slightly from machine to machine, but an overview will give you a general idea of what is involved.

It is important to understand the function of each control on your bread machine before starting to make a loaf of bread. Each feature may vary slightly between different machines, but they all work in a basically similar manner.

START AND STOP BUTTONS

The Start button initiates the whole process. Press it after you have placed all the ingredients required for the bread-making procedure in the bread pan and after you have selected all the required settings, such as loaf type, size, crust colour and delay timer.

The Stop button may actually be the same control or a separate one. Press it to stop the programme, either during the programme, if you need to override it, or at the end to turn off the machine. This cancels the "keep warm" cycle at the end of baking.

TIME DISPLAY AND STATUS INDICATOR

A window displays the time remaining until the end of the programme selected. In some machines the selected programme is also shown. Some models use this same window or a separate set of lights to indicate what is happening inside the machine. It gives information on whether the machine is on time delay, kneading, resting, rising, baking or warming.

PROGRAMME INDICATORS OR MENU

Each bread machine has a number of programmes for different types of bread. Some models have more than others. This function allows you to choose the appropriate programme for your recipe and indicates which one you have selected. These programmes are discussed in more detail later.

PRE-HEAT CYCLE

Some machines start all programmes with a warming phase, either prior to mixing or during the kneading phase. This feature can prove useful on colder days or when you are using larger quantities of ingredients, such as milk, straight from the refrigerator, as you do not have to wait for them to come to room temperature before making the bread.

DELAY TIMER

This button allows you to pre-set the bread machine to switch on automatically at a specified time. So, for example, you can have freshly baked bread for breakfast or when you return from work. The timer should not be used for dough that contains perishable ingredients such as fresh dairy products or meats, which deteriorate in a warm environment.

CRUST COLOUR CONTROL

The majority of bread machines have a default medium crust setting. If, however, you prefer a paler crust or the appearance of a high-bake loaf, most machines will give you the option of a lighter or darker crust. Breads high in sugar, or that contain eggs or cheese, may colour too much on a medium setting, so a lighter option may be preferable for these.

WARMING INDICATOR

When the bread has finished baking, it is best to remove it from the machine immediately. If for any reason this is not possible, the warming facility will switch on as soon as the bread is baked, to help prevent condensation of the steam, which otherwise would result in a soggy loaf. Most machines continue in this mode for an hour, some giving an audible reminder every few minutes to remove the bread.

LEFT: French Bread can be baked in the machine on a French bread setting, or the dough can be removed to make the traditional shape by hand.

MIXED FRUIT TEABREAD

When mixed dried fruits are plumped up by being soaked in orange juice before baking, the result is a succulent teabread which keeps well.

SMALL

75g/3oz/½ cup sultanas (golden raisins)

50g/2oz/⅓ cup raisins

25g/1oz/2 tbsp currants

15g/½oz/1 tbsp cut mixed (candied) peel

75g/3oz/6 tbsp soft light brown sugar

150ml/5fl oz/⅔ cup orange juice

1 egg, lightly beaten

65g/2½oz/generous ½ cup plain (all-purpose) white flour

65g/2½oz/generous ½ cup plain wholemeal (whole-wheat) flour

5ml/1 tsp baking powder

1.5ml/¼ tsp ground cinnamon

1.5ml/¼ tsp freshly grated nutmeg

MEDIUM

115g/4oz/⅔ cup sultanas

75g/3oz/½ cup raisins

40g/1½oz/3 tbsp currants

25g/1oz/2 tbsp cut mixed peel

115g/4oz/½ cup soft light brown sugar

200ml/7fl oz/⅞ cup orange juice

1 egg, lightly beaten

90g/3¼oz/generous ¾ cup plain white flour

90g/3¼oz/generous ¾ cup plain wholemeal flour

7.5ml/1½ tsp baking powder

2.5ml/½ tsp ground cinnamon

2.5ml/½ tsp freshly grated nutmeg

LARGE

175g/6oz/1 cup sultanas

125g/4½oz/¾ cup raisins

50g/2oz/¼ cup currants

25g/1oz/2 tbsp cut mixed peel

175g/6oz/¾ cup soft light brown sugar

300ml/10½fl oz/generous 1¼ cups orange juice

1 egg, lightly beaten

115g/4oz/1 cup plain white flour

115g/4oz/1 cup plain wholemeal flour

7.5ml/1½ tsp baking powder

2.5ml/½ tsp ground cinnamon

2.5ml/½ tsp freshly grated nutmeg

MAKES 1 TEABREAD

1 Place the dried fruit, peel and sugar in a bowl. Pour over the orange juice and leave to soak for 8 hours or overnight.

2 Remove the kneading blade from the bread pan and line the base of the pan with baking parchment or greased greaseproof (waxed) paper.

3 Add the egg, both types of flour, the baking powder, and spices to the fruit mixture and beat thoroughly to combine. Spoon the mixture into the prepared bread pan.

4 Set the machine to the "bake only" setting. Set the timer, if possible, for the recommended time. If not, set the timer and check the cake after the recommended time. Bake the small cake for 40–45 minutes, the medium for 55–60 minutes and the large cake for 75–80 minutes. Check after the shortest recommended time. It should be well risen and firm to the touch.

5 Remove the bread pan from the machine. Turn the cake out on to a wire rack after 2–3 minutes.

REMINDER LIGHTS

A few models are fitted with a set of lights which change colour after being activated, to serve as your reminder that certain essential steps have been followed. This helps to ensure that the kneading blade is fitted, and that basic ingredients such as liquid, flour and yeast have been placed in the bread pan.

LOAF SIZE

On larger bread machines you may have the option of making up to three different sizes of loaf. The actual sizes vary between individual machines, but approximate to small, medium and large loaves of around 450g/1lb, 675g/1½lb and 900g/2lb respectively. However, this control in some machines is for visual indication only and does not alter the baking time or cycle. Check the manufacturer's instructions.

BAKING PROGRAMMES

All machines have a selection of programmes to help ensure you produce the perfect loaf of bread. The lengths of kneading, rising and baking times are varied to suit the different flours and to determine the texture of the finished loaf.

BASIC OR NORMAL

This mode is the most commonly used programme, ideal for white loaves and mixed grain loaves where white bread flour is the main ingredient.

RAPID

This cycle reduces the time to make a standard loaf of bread by about 1 hour and is handy when speed is the main criterion. The finished loaf may not rise as much as one made on the basic programme and may therefore be a little more dense.

WHOLE WHEAT

This is a longer cycle than the basic one, to allow time for the slower rising action of doughs containing a high percentage of strong wholemeal (whole-wheat) flour. Some machines also have a multigrain mode for breads made with cereals and

ABOVE: Sun-dried tomatoes can be added to the dough at the raisin beep to make deliciously flavoured bread.

grains such as Granary and rye, although it is possible to make satisfactory breads using this or the basic mode, depending on the percentages of the flours.

FRENCH

This programme is best suited for low-fat and low-sugar breads, and it produces loaves with an open texture and crispier crust. More time within the cycle is devoted to rising, and in some bread machines the loaf is baked at a slightly higher temperature.

SWEET BREAD

A few bread machines offer this feature in addition to crust colour control. It is useful if you intend to bake breads with a high fat or sugar content which tend to colour too much.

CAKE

Again, this is a feature offered on a few machines. Some will mix a quick non-yeast teabread-type cake and then bake it; others will mix yeast-raised cakes. If you do not have this facility, teabreads and non-yeast cakes can easily be mixed in a bowl and cooked in the bread pan on a "bake only" cycle.

BAKE

This setting allows you to use the bread machine as an oven, either to bake cakes and ready-prepared dough from the supermarket or to extend the standard baking time if you prefer your bread to be particularly well done.

SANDWICH

This facility, which enables you to bake a loaf with a soft crust that is particularly suitable for sandwich slices, is available on one or two models only.

RAISIN BEEP

Additional ingredients can be added mid-cycle on most programmes. The machine gives an audible signal – usually a beep – and some machines pause late in the kneading phase so that ingredients such as fruit and nuts can be added. This late addition reduces the risk of them being crushed during the kneading phase.

If your machine does not have this facility, you can set a kitchen timer to ring 5 minutes before the end of the kneading cycle and add the extra ingredients then.

DOUGH PROGRAMMES

Most machines include a dough programme: some models have dough programmes with extra features.

DOUGH

This programme allows you to make dough without machine-baking it, which is essential for all hand-shaped breads. The machine mixes, kneads and proves the dough, ready for shaping, final proving and baking in a conventional oven. If you wish to make different shaped loaves or rolls, buns and pastries, you will find this facility invaluable.

OTHER DOUGH PROGRAMMES

Some machines include cycles for making different types of dough, such as a rapid dough mode for pizzas and Focaccia or a longer mode for wholemeal dough and bagel dough. Some "dough only" cycles also include the raisin beep facility.

RASPBERRY AND ALMOND TEABREAD

Fresh raspberries and almonds combine perfectly to flavour this mouthwatering cake. Toasted flaked almonds make a crunchy topping.

1 Remove the kneading blade from the bread pan and line the base of the pan with baking parchment or greased greaseproof (waxed) paper.

2 Sift the self-raising flour into a large bowl. Add the butter and rub in with your fingertips until the mixture resembles fine breadcrumbs.

3 Stir in the caster sugar and ground almonds. Gradually beat in the egg(s). If making the small or large teabread, beat in the milk.

4 Fold in the raspberries, then spoon the mixture into the prepared tin. Sprinkle over the flaked almonds.

SMALL
140g/5oz/1¼ cups self-raising (self-rising) flour
70g/2½oz/5 tbsp butter, cut into pieces
70g/2½oz/generous ⅓ cup caster (superfine) sugar
25g/1oz/¼ cup ground almonds
1 egg, lightly beaten
30ml/2 tbsp milk
115g/4oz/1 cup raspberries
22ml/1½ tbsp toasted flaked (sliced) almonds

MEDIUM
175g/6oz/1½ cups self-raising flour
90g/3½oz/7 tbsp butter, cut into pieces
90g/3½oz/½ cup caster sugar
40g/1½oz/⅓ cup ground almonds
2 eggs, lightly beaten
140g/5oz/1¼ cups raspberries
30ml/2 tbsp toasted flaked almonds

LARGE
225g/8oz/2 cups self-raising flour
115g/4oz/½ cup butter, cut into pieces
115g/4oz/generous ½ cup caster sugar
50g/2oz/½ cup ground almonds
2 eggs, lightly beaten
45ml/3 tbsp milk
175g/6oz/1½ cups raspberries
30ml/2 tbsp toasted flaked almonds

MAKES 1 TEABREAD

5 Set the bread machine to the "bake only" setting. Set the timer, if possible, for the recommended time. If not, set the timer and check after the shortest recommended time. Bake the small teabread for 35–40 minutes, the medium for 45–50 minutes and the large cake for 65–70 minutes or until well risen.

6 Test by inserting a skewer into the centre of the teabread. It should come out clean. If necessary, bake for a few minutes more. Then remove the pan from the machine. Turn out on to a wire rack to cool after 2–3 minutes.

BAKING, COOLING AND STORING

A bread machine should always bake a perfect loaf of bread, but it is important to remember that it is just a machine and cannot think for itself. It is essential that you measure the ingredients carefully and add them to the bread pan in the order specified by the manufacturer of your machine. Ingredients should be at room temperature, so take them out of the refrigerator in good time, unless your machine has a pre-heat cycle.

Check the dough during the kneading cycles; if your machine does not have a window, open the lid and look into the bread pan. The dough should be slightly tacky to the touch. If it is very soft add a little more flour; if the dough feels very firm and dry add a little more liquid. It is also worth checking the dough towards the end of the rising period. On particularly warm days your bread may rise too high. If this happens it may rise over the bread pan and begin to travel down the outside during the first few minutes of baking. If your bread looks ready for baking before the baking cycle is due to begin, you have two options. You can either override and cancel the programme, then re-programme using a "bake only" cycle, or you can try pricking the top of the loaf with a cocktail stick (toothpick) to deflate it slightly and let the programme continue.

Different machines will give different browning levels using the same recipe. Check when you try a new recipe and make a note to select a lighter or darker setting next time if necessary.

BELOW: Use a cocktail stick to prick dough that has risen too high.

REMOVING THE BREAD FROM THE PAN

Once the bread is baked it is best removed from the bread pan immediately. Turn the bread pan upside down, holding it with oven gloves or a thick protective cloth – it will be very hot – and shake it several times to release the bread. If removing the bread is difficult, rap the corner of the bread pan on a wooden board several times or try turning the base of the shaft underneath the base of the bread pan. Don't try to free the bread by using a knife or similar metal object, or you will scratch the non-stick coating.

If the kneading blade remains inside the loaf, you should use a heat-resistant plastic or wooden implement to prise it out. The metal blade and the bread will be too hot to use your fingers.

ABOVE: Multigrain Bread is made with honey which, like other sweeteners, acts as a preservative. The loaf should stay moist for longer.

BELOW: Use a serrated bread knife when slicing bread so that you do not damage the texture of the crumb.

Baking, Cooling and Storing

COCONUT CAKE

Desiccated coconut gives this simple, speedy cake a wonderful moist texture and delectable aroma.

SMALL

75g/3oz/6 tbsp butter or margarine, softened
115g/4oz/generous ½ cup caster (superfine) sugar
2 eggs, lightly beaten
115g/4oz/1⅓ cups desiccated (dry unsweetened shredded) coconut
85g/3oz/¾ cup self-raising (self-rising) flour
55ml/2fl oz/¼ cup sour cream
5ml/1 tsp grated lemon rind

MEDIUM

100g/3½oz/7 tbsp butter or margarine, softened
140g/5oz/¾ cup caster sugar
2 large eggs, lightly beaten
140g/5oz/1⅔ cups desiccated coconut
100g/3½oz/scant 1 cup self-raising flour
70ml/2½fl oz/scant ⅓ cup sour cream
7.5ml/1½ tsp grated lemon rind

LARGE

115g/4oz/½ cup butter or margarine, softened
175g/6oz/scant 1 cup caster sugar
3 eggs, lightly beaten
175g/6oz/2 cups desiccated coconut
115g/4oz/1 cup self-raising flour
85ml/3fl oz/⅜ cup sour cream
10ml/2 tsp grated lemon rind

MAKES 1 CAKE

1 Remove the kneading blade from the bread pan and line the base of the pan with baking parchment.

2 Cream the butter or margarine and sugar together until pale and fluffy, then add the eggs a little at a time, beating well after each addition.

3 Add the desiccated coconut, flour, sour cream and lemon rind. Gradually mix together, using a non-metallic spoon.

4 Spoon into the pan. Set the machine to the "bake only" setting. Set the timer, if possible, for the recommended time. If not, set the timer and check after the shortest recommended time. Bake the small or medium cake for 45–50 minutes and the large cake for 65–70 minutes.

5 Test by inserting a skewer into the centre of the cake. It should come out clean. If necessary, bake for a few minutes more.

6 Remove the bread pan from the machine. Let stand for 2–3 minutes, then turn the cake out on to a wire rack to cool.

COOK'S TIP
This is delicious with a lemon syrup drizzled over the cooked cake. Heat 30ml/2 tbsp lemon juice with 100g/3½oz/scant ½ cup granulated sugar and 85ml/3fl oz/6 tbsp water in a pan, stirring until the sugar has dissolved. Bring to the boil, then simmer for 2–3 minutes before drizzling the syrup over the warm coconut cake.

COOLING

Place the bread on a wire rack to allow the steam to escape and leave it for at least 30 minutes before slicing. Always slice bread using a serrated knife to avoid damaging the crumb structure.

STORING

Cool the bread, then wrap it in foil or place it in a plastic bag and seal it, to preserve the freshness. If your bread has a crisp crust, this will soften on storage, so until it is sliced it is best left uncovered. After cutting, put the loaf in a large paper bag, but try to use it fairly quickly, as bread starts to dry out as soon as it is cut. Breads containing eggs tend to dry out even more quickly, while those made with honey or added fats stay moist for longer.

BELOW: Parker House Rolls can be frozen after baking, as soon as they are cool. They taste delicious warm, so refresh them in the oven just before serving.

ABOVE: If you are freezing bread to be used for toasting, slice the loaf first.

Ideally, freshly baked bread should be consumed within 2–3 days. Avoid storing bread in the fridge as this causes it to go stale more quickly.

Freeze cooked breads if you need to keep them for longer. Place the loaf or rolls in a freezer bag, seal and freeze for up to 3 months. If you intend to use the bread for toast or sandwiches, it is easier

ABOVE: Store bread with a crispy crust in a large paper bag.

to slice it before freezing, so you can remove only the number of slices you need. Thaw the bread at room temperature, still in its freezer bag.

With some loaves, however, freezing may not be a sensible option. For example, very crusty bread, such as French Couronne, tends to come apart after it has been frozen and thawed.

STORING BREAD DOUGHS

If it is not convenient to bake bread dough immediately you can store it in an oiled bowl which has been covered with clear film, or seal it in a plastic bag. Dough can be stored in the refrigerator for up to 2 days if it contains butter, milk or eggs and up to 4 days if no perishable ingredients are included.

Keep an eye on the dough and knock it back occasionally. When you are ready to use the dough, bring it back to room temperature, then shape, prove and bake it in the normal way.

You can make dough in your machine, shape it, then keep it in the refrigerator overnight, ready for baking conventionally next morning for breakfast. Cover with oiled clear film as usual.

Bread dough can be frozen in a freezerproof bag for up to 1 month. When you are ready to use it, thaw the dough overnight in the refrigerator or at room temperature for 2–3 hours. Once the dough has thawed, place it in a warm place to rise, but remember it will take longer to rise than freshly made dough.

ABOVE: Store dough in the refrigerator in an oiled bowl covered in clear film (plastic wrap) or in a plastic bag.

ABOVE: Prepare rolls the night before and store in the refrigerator, ready to bake the following morning.

Baking, Cooling and Storing

GINGERBREAD

This tea-time favourite can be baked easily in your bread machine. Store it in an airtight tin for a couple of days to allow the characteristic moist sticky texture to develop fully.

SMALL

*175g/6oz/1½ cups plain
(all-purpose) flour
3.5ml/¾ tsp ground ginger
5ml/1 tsp baking powder
1.5ml/¼ tsp bicarbonate of soda
(baking soda)
2.5ml/½ tsp mixed (apple pie) spice
75g/3oz/6 tbsp light muscovado
(brown) sugar
50g/2oz/¼ cup butter, cut into pieces
75g/3oz/scant ⅓ cup golden
(light corn) syrup
40g/1½oz black treacle (molasses)
105ml/7 tbsp milk
1 egg, lightly beaten
40g/1½oz/¼ cup drained preserved
stem ginger, thinly sliced*

MEDIUM

*225g/8oz/2 cups plain flour
5ml/1 tsp ground ginger
7.5ml/1½ tsp baking powder
2.5ml/½ tsp bicarbonate of soda
2.5ml/½ tsp mixed spice
115g/4oz/½ cup light muscovado sugar
75g/3oz/6 tbsp butter, cut into pieces
100g/3½oz/generous ⅓ cup
golden syrup
50g/2oz black treacle
150ml/5fl oz/⅔ cup milk
1 egg, lightly beaten
50g/2oz/⅓ cup drained preserved
stem ginger, thinly sliced*

1 Remove the blade from the bread pan and line the base with baking parchment or greased greaseproof (waxed) paper. Sift the flour, ginger, baking powder, bicarbonate of soda and mixed spice together into a large bowl.

2 Melt the sugar, butter, syrup and treacle in a pan over a low heat.

3 Make a well in the centre of the dry ingredients and pour in the melted mixture. Add the milk, egg and stem ginger and mix thoroughly.

4 Pour the mixture into the bread pan and set the machine to the "bake only" setting. Set the timer, if possible, for the recommended time. If not, set the timer and check the gingerbread after the shortest recommended time. Bake the small gingerbread for 45–50 minutes, the medium for 50–55 minutes and the large for 65–70 minutes, or until well risen.

5 Remove the bread pan from the machine. Let stand for 2–3 minutes, then turn the gingerbread out on to a wire rack to cool.

LARGE

*280g/10oz/2½ cups plain flour
7.5ml/1½ tsp ground ginger
10ml/2 tsp baking powder
3.5ml/¾ tsp bicarbonate of soda
3.5ml/¾ tsp mixed spice
125g/4½oz/generous ½ cup light
muscovado sugar
115g/4oz/½ cup butter, cut into pieces
125g/4½oz/scant ½ cup golden syrup
50g/2oz black treacle
200ml/7fl oz/⅞ cup milk
1 egg, lightly beaten
50g/2oz/⅓ cup drained preserved
stem ginger, thinly sliced*

MAKES 1 LOAF

HAND-SHAPED LOAVES

One of the most useful features a bread machine can have is the dough setting. Use this, and the machine will automatically mix the ingredients, and will then knead and rest the dough before providing the ideal conditions for it to rise for the first time. The whole cycle, from mixing through to rising, takes around 1¾ hours, but remember it will vary slightly between machines.

KNOCKING BACK

1 At the end of the cycle, the dough will have almost doubled in bulk and will be ready for shaping. Remove the bread pan from the machine.

2 Lightly flour a work surface. Gently remove the dough from the bread pan and place it on the floured surface. Knock back (punch down) the dough to relieve the tension in the gluten and expel some of the carbon dioxide.

3 Knead the dough lightly for about 1–2 minutes; shape into a tight ball. At this stage, a recipe may suggest you cover the dough with oiled clear film (plastic wrap) and leave it to rest for a few minutes. This allows the gluten to relax so dough will be easier to handle.

SHAPING

Techniques to shape dough vary, depending on the finished form of the bread you wish to make. The following steps illustrate how to form basic bread, roll and yeast pastry shapes.

BAGUETTE

1 To shape a baguette or French stick, flatten the dough into a rectangle about 2.5cm/1in thick, either using the palms of your hands or a rolling pin.

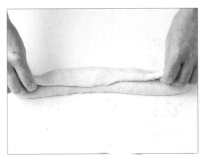

2 From one long side fold one-third of the dough down and then fold over the remaining third of dough and press gently to secure. Repeat twice more, resting the dough in between folds to avoid tearing.

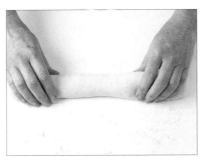

3 Gently stretch the dough and roll it backwards and forwards with your hands to make a breadstick of even thickness and the required length.

4 Place the baguette dough between a folded floured dish towel, or in a banneton, and leave in a warm place to prove. The dish towel or banneton will help the baguette to keep the correct shape as it rises.

BLOOMER

1 Roll the dough out to a rectangle 2.5cm/1in thick. Roll up from one long side and place it, seam side up, on a floured baking sheet. Cover and leave to rest for 15 minutes.

2 Turn the loaf over and place on another floured baking sheet. Using your fingertips, tuck the sides and ends of the dough under. Cover; leave to finish rising.

TIN LOAF

Roll the dough out to a rectangle the length of the tin (pan) and three times as wide. Fold the dough widthways, bringing the top third down and the bottom third up. Press the dough down, turn it over and place it in the tin.

HONEY CAKE

If you like the taste of honey, you are sure to love this cake. Serve it with tea or coffee or as a dessert with fresh fruit and crème fraîche.

Small
40g/1½oz/3 tbsp butter
100ml/3½fl oz/7 tbsp clear honey
75g/3oz/¾ cup plain
(all-purpose) flour
pinch of salt
5ml/1 tsp baking powder
2.5ml/½ tsp bicarbonate of soda
(baking soda)
2.5ml/½ tsp mixed (apple pie) spice
75g/3oz/¾ cups wholemeal
(whole-wheat) flour
15ml/1 tbsp milk
1 egg, lightly beaten
30ml/2 tbsp thick-cut marmalade

Medium
50g/2oz/¼ cup butter
150ml/5fl oz/⅔ cup clear honey
115g/4oz/1 cup plain flour
pinch of salt
7.5ml/1½ tsp baking powder
2.5ml/½ tsp bicarbonate of soda
5ml/1 tsp mixed spice
115g/4oz/1 cup wholemeal flour
2 eggs, lightly beaten
45ml/3 tbsp thick-cut marmalade

Large
65g/2½oz/5 tbsp butter
180ml/6½fl oz/generous ¾ cup
clear honey
140g/5oz/1¼ cups plain flour
pinch of salt
10ml/2 tsp baking powder
3.5ml/¾ tsp bicarbonate of soda
5ml/1 tsp mixed spice
140g/5oz/1¼ cups wholemeal flour
15ml/1 tbsp milk
2 eggs, lightly beaten
60ml/4 tbsp thick-cut marmalade

MAKES 1 CAKE

1 Remove the kneading blade from the bread pan and line the base of the pan with baking parchment or greased greaseproof (waxed) paper.

2 Place the butter and honey in a small pan and heat gently, stirring all the time until the butter has melted.

3 Sift the plain flour, salt, baking powder, bicarbonate of soda and mixed spice into a mixing bowl. Stir in the wholemeal flour.

4 Stir the milk, if using, into the beaten egg, if making the small or large cake. Gradually pour on to the flour mixture, alternately with the honey and butter mixture, beating well after each addition of liquid.

5 Spoon the mixture into the prepared bread pan. Set the bread machine to the "bake only" setting. Set the timer, if possible, for the recommended time. If not, set the timer and check the cake after the shortest recommended time. Bake the small cake for 35–40 minutes, the medium cake for 40–45 minutes and the large cake for 50–55 minutes, or until well risen and firm to the touch.

6 Test by inserting a skewer into the centre of the cake. It should come out clean. If necessary, bake the cake for a few minutes more.

7 Remove the pan from the machine. Leave it to stand for 2–3 minutes, then turn the cake out on to a wire rack.

8 Melt the marmalade in a small pan and brush it over the warm cake, to glaze.

COTTAGE LOAF

1 To shape a cottage loaf, divide the dough into two pieces, approximately one-third and two-thirds in size. Shape each piece of dough into a plump round ball and place on lightly floured baking sheets. Cover with inverted bowls and leave to rise for 30 minutes, or until 50 per cent larger.

2 Flatten the top of the large loaf. Using a sharp knife, cut a cross about 4cm/1½in across in the centre. Brush the area lightly with water and place the small round on top.

3 Using one or two fingers or the floured handle of a wooden spoon, press the centre of the top round, penetrating into the middle of the dough beneath.

TWIST

1 To shape bread for a twist, divide the dough into two equal pieces. Using the palms of your hands, roll each piece of dough on a lightly floured surface into a long rope, about 4–5cm/1½–2in thick. Make both ropes the same length.

2 Place the two ropes side by side. Starting from the centre, twist one rope over the other. Continue in the same way until you reach the end, then pinch the ends together and tuck the join underneath. Turn the dough around and repeat the process with the other end, twisting the dough in the same direction as the first.

BREADSTICK

To shape a breadstick, roll the dough to a rectangle about 1cm/½in thick, and cut out strips that are about 7.5cm/3in long and 2cm/¾in wide. Using the palm of your hand, gently roll each strip into a long thin rope.

It may help to lift each rope and pull it very gently to stretch it. If you are still finding it difficult to stretch the dough, leave it to rest for a few minutes and then try again.

COURONNE

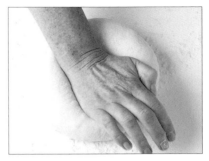

1 Shape the dough into a ball. Using the heal of your hand make a hole in the centre. Gradually enlarge the centre, turning the dough to make a circle, with a 13cm 15cm/5–6in cavity.

2 Place on a lightly oiled baking sheet. Put a small, lightly oiled bowl in the centre of the ring to prevent the dough from filling in the centre during rising.

SCROLL

Roll out the dough using your palms, until it forms a rope, about 25cm/10in long, with tapered ends. Form into a loose "S" shape, then curl the ends in to make a scroll. Leave a small space to allow for the final proving (rising).

CRUNCHY PEAR AND CHERRY CAKE

Made from quick all-in-one cake mixture and filled with juicy pears and cherries, this cake has a crunchy demerara topping which contrasts beautifully with the soft crumb.

1 Remove the kneading blade from the bread pan and line the base of the pan with non-stick baking paper or greased greaseproof (waxed) paper.

2 Mix the margarine and caster sugar in a large bowl. Add the eggs, milk, flour and baking powder. Beat together for 1–2 minutes. Fold in the pears, cherries and ginger, using a metal spoon.

3 Spoon the mixture into the prepared pan and sprinkle half the demerara sugar over the top. Set the machine to the "bake only" setting. Set the timer, if possible, for the recommended time. If not, set the timer and check the cake after the shortest recommended time. Bake the small cake for 45–50 minutes, the medium cake for 50–55 minutes and the large cake for 65–70 minutes.

4 Sprinkle the remaining sugar over after 25 minutes if baking the small cake, after 30 minutes if baking the medium cake, and after 35 minutes if baking the large cake.

5 Remove the bread pan from the machine. Leave the cake to stand for 2–3 minutes, then turn out on to a wire rack to cool.

SMALL
75g/3oz/6 tbsp soft margarine
75g/3oz/scant ½ cup caster (superfine) sugar
2 eggs
30ml/2 tbsp milk
170g/6oz/1½ cups plain (all-purpose) flour
7.5ml/1½ tsp baking powder
50g/2oz/½ cup ready-to-eat dried pears, chopped
40g/1½oz/2 tbsp glacé (candied) cherries, quartered
25g/1oz/2 tbsp crystallized (candied) ginger, chopped
22ml/1½ tbsp demerara (raw) sugar

MEDIUM
100g/3½oz/7 tbsp soft margarine
100g/3½oz/½ cup caster sugar
2 eggs
60ml/4 tbsp milk
225g/8oz/2 cups plain flour
10ml/2 tsp baking powder
65g/2½oz/generous ½ cup ready-to-eat dried pears, chopped
65g/2½oz/generous ¼ cup glacé cherries, quartered
40g/1½oz/3 tbsp crystallized ginger, chopped
30ml/2 tbsp demerara sugar

LARGE
140g/5oz/⅔ cup soft margarine
140g/5oz/¾ cup caster sugar
3 eggs
60ml/4 tbsp milk
280g/10oz/2½ cups plain flour
12.5ml/2½ tsp baking powder
75g/3oz/¾ cup ready-to-eat dried pears, chopped
75g/3oz/scant ½ cup glacé cherries, quartered
50g/2oz/4 tbsp crystallized ginger, chopped
30ml/2 tbsp demerara sugar

MAKES 1 CAKE

CROISSANT

1 To shape a croissant, roll out the dough on a lightly floured surface and then cut it into strips that are about 15cm/6in wide.

2 Cut each strip along its length into triangles with 15cm/6in bases and 18cm/7in sides.

3 Place with the pointed end towards you and the 15cm/6in base at the top; gently pull each corner of the base to stretch it slightly.

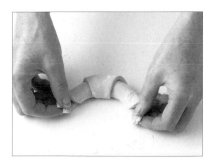

4 Roll up the dough with one hand from the base while pulling, finishing with the dough point underneath. Finally, curve the corners around in the direction of the pointed end to make the curved croissant shape.

BRAIDED ROLL

1 To shape a braided roll, place the dough on a lightly floured surface and roll out. Divide the dough into balls, the number depending on the amount of dough and how many rolls you would like to make.

2 Divide each ball of dough into three equal pieces. Using your hands, roll into long, thin ropes of equal length and place them side by side.

3 Pinch one of the ends together and braid the pieces of dough. Finally, pinch the remaining ends together and then tuck the join under.

FILLED BRAIDED LOAF

1 Place the dough for the braided loaf on a lightly floured surface. Roll out and shape into a rectangle. Using a sharp knife, make diagonal cuts down each of the long sides of the dough, about 2cm/⅔in wide. Place the filling in the centre of the uncut strip.

2 Fold in the end strip of dough, then fold over alternate strips of dough to form a braid over the filling. Tuck in the final end to seal the braid.

PROVING

After the dough has been shaped, it will need to be left to rise again. This is sometimes referred to as proving the dough. Most doughs are left in a warm place until they just about double in bulk. How long this takes will vary – depending on the ambient temperature and richness of the dough – but somewhere between 30 and 60 minutes is usual.

Avoid leaving dough to rise for too long (over-proving) or it may collapse in the oven or when it is slashed before baking. Equally, you need to leave it to rise sufficiently, or the finished loaf will be heavy.

To test if the dough is ready to bake, press it lightly with your fingertip; it should feel springy, not firm. The indentation made by your finger should slowly fill and spring back.

ABOVE: A dough that has been shaped and placed in a bread tin (pan) to rise. The unproved dough should reach just over halfway up the tin.

ABOVE: Leave the dough in a warm, draught-free place to rise. This should take between 30 and 60 minutes. Once risen, the dough will have almost doubled in bulk.

MADEIRA CAKE

Delicately flavoured with vanilla, this classic plain cake has a firm yet light texture. Serve the traditional way with a glass of its namesake.

SMALL
115g/4oz/½ cup butter, cut into pieces
115g/4oz/generous ½ cup caster (superfine) sugar
a few drops vanilla essence (extract)
125g/4½oz/1 cup self-raising (self-rising) flour
40g/1½oz/6 tbsp plain (all-purpose) flour
2 eggs, lightly beaten
15–30ml/1–2 tbsp milk

MEDIUM
140g/5oz/⅔ cup butter, cut into pieces
140g/5oz/¾ cup caster sugar
1.5ml/¼ tsp vanilla essence
165g/5½oz/generous 1¼ cups self-raising flour
40g/1½oz/6 tbsp plain flour
3 eggs, lightly beaten
15–30ml/1–2 tbsp milk

LARGE
175g/6oz/¾ cup butter, cut into pieces
175g/6oz/⅞ cup caster sugar
1.5ml/¼ tsp vanilla essence
175g/6oz/1½ cups self-raising flour
50g/2oz/½ cup plain (all-purpose) flour
3 eggs, lightly beaten
15–30ml/1–2 tbsp milk

MAKES 1 CAKE

1 Prepare the machine. Remove the kneading blade from the bread pan and line the base with baking parchment.

2 Cream the butter and sugar together until the mixture is very light and fluffy, then beat in the vanilla essence.

3 Sift the flours together. Gradually beat the eggs into the creamed mixture, beating well after each addition, and adding a little flour if the mixture starts to curdle.

COOK'S TIP

Cakes cooked in a bread pan tend to have browner sides than when cooked conventionally, in an oven, as the cooking element is around the sides of the bread pan. Cakes such as this, which have a high proportion of fat and sugar, need to be watched closely, as the edges will easily overcook.

4 Fold in the remaining flour mixture, using a metal spoon, then add enough of the milk to give a dropping consistency.

5 Spoon the mixture into the prepared bread pan and set the bread machine on the "bake only" setting. Set the timer, if possible, for the recommended time. If, on your bread machine, the minimum time on the "bake only" setting is for longer than the time suggested here, set the timer and check the cake after the shortest recommended time. Bake the small madeira cake for 40–45 minutes, the medium for 45–50 minutes and the large cake for 55–60 minutes.

6 The cake should be well risen and firm to the touch. Test by inserting a skewer into the centre of the cake. It should come out clean. If necessary, bake for a few minutes more.

7 Remove the bread pan from the machine. Leave it to stand for about 2–3 minutes, then turn the madeira cake out on to a wire rack to cool.

SLASHING

Slashing bread dough before baking serves a useful purpose as well as adding a decorative finish, as found on the tops of traditional loaf shapes such as bloomers and French sticks. When the dough goes into the oven it has one final rise, known as "oven spring", so the cuts or slashes allow the bread to expand without tearing or cracking the sides.

The earlier you slash the dough the wider the splits will be. Depth is important, too: the deeper the slashes the more the bread will open during baking. Most recipes suggest slashing just before glazing and baking. If you think a bread has slightly over proved keep the slashes fairly shallow and gentle to avoid the possibility of the dough collapsing.

Use a sharp knife or scalpel blade to make a clean cut. Move smoothly and swiftly to avoid tearing the dough. Scissors can also be used to make an easy decorative finish to rolls or breads.

SLASHING A SPLIT TIN OR FARMHOUSE LOAF

A long slash, about 1cm/½in deep, can be made along the top of the dough just before baking. You can use this slashing procedure for both machine and hand-shaped loaves. Using a very sharp knife, plunge into one end of the dough and pull the blade smoothly along the entire length, but make sure you do not drag the dough.

If flouring the top of the loaf, sprinkle with flour before slashing.

SLASHING A BAGUETTE

To slash a baguette, cut long slashes of equal length and depth four or five times along its length. A razor-sharp blade is the best tool for slashing breads. Used with care, a scalpel is perfectly safe and has the advantage that the blades can be changed to ensure you always have a sharp edge.

USING SCISSORS TO SLASH ROLLS

Rolls can be given quick and interesting finishes using a pair of sharp-pointed scissors. You could experiment with all sorts of ideas. Try the following to start you off.

• Just before baking cut across the top of the dough first in one direction then the other to make a cross.

• Make six horizontal or vertical cuts equally spaced around the sides of the rolls. Leave for 5 minutes before baking.

• Cut through the rolls in four or five places from the edge almost to the centre, just before baking.

ABOVE: Top rolls: making a cross; middle rolls: horizontal cuts around the side; bottom rolls: cuts from the edge almost to the centre.

BAKING BREAD WITH A CRISP CRUST

For a crisper crust, it is necessary to introduce steam into the oven. The moisture initially softens the dough, so that it can rise, resulting in a crispier crust. Moisture also improves the crust colour by encouraging caramelization of the natural sugars in the dough. Standing the loaf on a baking stone or unglazed terracotta tiles also helps to produce a crisp crust, the effect being similar to when breads are cooked in a clay or brick oven. The porous tiles or stone hold heat and draw moisture from the bread base while it is baking.

1 About 30 minutes before you intend to bake, place the baking stone on the bottom shelf of the oven, then preheat the oven. Alternatively line the oven shelf with unglazed terracotta tiles, leaving air space all around to allow for the free circulation of the hot air.

2 When ready to bake, using a peel (baker's shovel), place the bread directly on the tiles or baking stone.

3 Using a water spray bottle, mist the oven walls two or three times during the first 5–10 minutes of baking. Open the oven door as little as possible, spray the oven walls and quickly close the door to avoid unnecessary heat loss. Remember not to spray the oven light, fan or heating elements.

TEABREADS & CAKES

Traditional teabreads and cakes use baking powder rather than yeast as a raising agent, giving them a light texture and a good flavour. Classic cakes, such as Madeira Cake, Marble Cake and Gingerbread can easily be baked in a bread machine. For more exotic combinations, there are recipes for Strawberry Teabread, flavoured with ground hazelnuts; fresh Raspberry and Almond Teabread or sugar-topped Crunchy Pear and Cherry Cake.

GLAZES

Both machine-baked breads and hand-shaped loaves benefit from a glaze to give that final finishing touch. Glazes may be used before baking, or during the early stages of baking to give a more golden crust or to change its texture of the crust. This is particularly noticeable with hand-shaped breads but good results may also be obtained with machine-baked loaves. Glazes may also be applied after baking to give flavour and a glossy finish. Another important role for glazes is to act as an adhesive, to help any topping applied to the loaf stick to the surface of the dough.

For machine-baked breads, the glaze should either be brushed on to the loaf just before the baking cycle commences, or within 10 minutes of the start of the baking cycle. Apply the glaze quickly, so there is minimal heat loss while the bread machine lid is open. Avoid brushing the edges of the loaf with a sticky glaze as this might make the bread stick to the pan.

Glazes using egg, milk and salted water can also be brushed over freshly cooked loaves. Brush the glaze over as soon as the baking cycle finishes, then leave the bread inside the machine for 3–4 minutes, to allow the glaze to dry to a shine. Then remove the loaf from the machine and pan in the usual way. This method is useful if you want to sprinkle over a topping.

For hand-shaped loaves, you can brush with glaze before or after baking, and some recipes, such as Parker House Rolls will suggest that you do both.

GLAZES USED BEFORE OR DURING BAKING

For a crust with an attractive glossy shine, apply a glaze before or during baking.

MILK

Brush on loaves, such as potato breads, where a softer golden crust is desired. Milk is also used for bridge rolls, buns (such as teacakes) and flatbreads where a soft crust is desirable. It can also be used on baps and soft morning rolls before dusting with flour.

OLIVE OIL

This is mainly used with Continental-style breads, such as focaccia, stromboli and fougasse. It adds flavour and a shiny finish; and the darker the oil the fuller the flavour, so use extra virgin olive oil for a really deep taste. Olive oil can be used before and/or after baking.

BELOW: French Fougasse is brushed with olive oil just before baking.

BUTTER

Rolls and buns are brushed with melted butter before baking to add colour, while also keeping the dough soft. American Parker House Rolls are brushed before and after baking, while corn bread is often drizzled with melted butter before being baked. Butter adds a rich flavour to the breads glazed with it.

SALTED WATER

Mix 10ml/2 tsp salt with 30ml/2 tbsp water and brush over the dough immediately before baking. This gives a crisp baked crust with a slight sheen.

EGG WHITE

Use 1 egg white mixed with 15ml/1 tbsp water for a lighter golden, slightly shiny crust. This is often a better alternative to egg yolk for savoury breads.

EGG YOLK

Mix 1 egg yolk with 15ml/1 tbsp milk or water. This classic glaze, also known as egg wash, is used to give a golden, shiny crust. For sweet buns, breads and yeast cakes add 15ml/1 tbsp caster (superfine) sugar, for extra colour and flavour.

SPICED FRUIT KUGELHOPF

Sultanas steeped in spiced rum flavour this brioche-style bread, which is baked in a special fluted mould with a central funnel.

1 Mix the rum, ginger, cloves, cinnamon stick and nutmeg in a small pan and place over a medium heat until hot, but not bubbling. Remove from the heat, add the sultanas and set aside in the pan for 30 minutes.

2 Pour the milk into the machine pan. Add three of the eggs, then separate the remaining eggs, setting the whites aside, and add the egg yolks to the pan.

3 Remove the cloves and cinnamon from the pan and discard (although the cinnamon stick can be dried for re-use later). Place a sieve over the bread pan and drain the sultanas in it so that the juices fall through into the pan. Set the sultanas aside. If the instructions for your bread machine specify that the yeast is to be placed in the machine pan first, then simply reverse the order in which you add the liquid and dry ingredients to the pan.

4 Sprinkle over the flour, ensuring that it covers the liquid mixture completely. Add the salt and sugar in separate corners of the bread pan. Make a small indent in the centre of the flour (but not down as far as the liquid) and add the easy-blend dried yeast.

5 Set the bread machine to the dough setting; use basic dough setting (if available). Press Start. Mix for 5 minutes, then gradually add the melted butter. Lightly oil a non-stick kugelhopf tin.

6 When the dough cycle has finished, put the dough in a large mixing bowl. In a separate, grease-free bowl, whisk the egg whites to soft peaks. Add the reserved sultanas and cut mixed peel to the dough and fold in, using your hands. Gradually fold in the egg whites to form a soft dough.

7 Spoon the dough into the kugelhopf tin in three or four batches, making sure it is evenly distributed. Cover with lightly oiled clear film (plastic wrap) and leave in a slightly warm place for 1–1½ hours, or until the dough has risen and is almost at the top of the tin.

8 Preheat the oven to 190°C/375°F/Gas 5. Bake the kugelhopf for 50–60 minutes or until it has browned and is firm to the touch. You can cover the surface with baking parchment if it starts to brown too quickly. Turn out on to a wire rack to cool. Dust with icing sugar.

100ml/3½fl oz/7 tbsp dark rum
5ml/1 tsp ground ginger
3 whole cloves
1 cinnamon stick
5ml/1 tsp freshly grated nutmeg
115g/4oz/⅔ cup sultanas
(golden raisins)
30ml/2 tbsp milk
5 eggs
500g/1lb 2oz/4½ cups unbleached
white bread flour
2.5ml/½ tsp salt
75g/3oz/6 tbsp caster
(superfine) sugar
10ml/2 tsp easy-blend (rapid-rise)
dried yeast
75g/3oz/6 tbsp butter, melted
75g/3oz/½ cup cut mixed
(candied) peel
icing (confectioners') sugar,
for dusting

MAKES 1 LOAF

GLAZES ADDED AFTER BAKING

Some glazes are used after baking, often on sweet breads, cakes and pastries. These glazes generally give a glossy and/or sticky finish, and also help to keep the bread or cake moist. They are suited to both machine and hand-shaped breads.

BUTTER

Breads such as Italian panettone and stollen are brushed with melted butter after baking to soften the crust. Clarified butter is also sometimes used as a glaze to soften flatbreads such as Naan.

HONEY, MALT, MOLASSES AND GOLDEN SYRUP

Liquid sweeteners can be warmed and brushed over breads, rolls, teabreads and cakes to give a soft, sweet, sticky crust. Honey is a traditional glaze and provides a lovely flavour, for example. Both malt and molasses have quite a strong flavour, so use these sparingly, matching them to compatible breads such as fruit loaves and cakes. Or you could mix them with a milder-flavoured liquid sweetener, such as golden syrup, to reduce their impact slightly.

SUGAR GLAZE

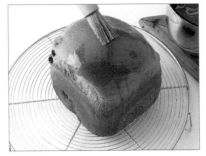

Dissolve 30–45ml/2–3 tbsp granulated sugar in the same amount of milk or water. Bring to the boil then simmer for 1–2 minutes, until syrupy. Brush over fruit loaves or buns for a glossy sheen. For extra flavour, use rose water.

SYRUPS

Yeast cakes, such as Savarin, are often drizzled with sugar syrup, flavoured with liqueurs, spirits or lemon juice. The syrup moistens the bread, while adding a decorative topping at the same time.

PRESERVES

Jam or marmalade can be melted with a little liquid. Choose water, liqueur, spirits (such as rum or brandy) or fruit juice, depending on the bread to be glazed. The liquid thins the preserve and adds flavour. It can be brushed over freshly baked warm teabreads, Danish pastries and sweet breads to a give a glossy, sticky finish. Dried fruit and nuts can then be sprinkled on top.

Select a flavoured jam to complement your bread or teacake. If in doubt, use apricot jam.

ICING SUGAR GLAZE

Mix 30–45ml/2–3 tbsp icing (confectioner's) sugar with 15ml/1 tbsp fruit juice, milk, single (light) cream or water and drizzle or brush over warm sweet breads, cakes and pastries. Add a pinch of spice to the icing sugar to bring out the flavour of the loaf. Maple syrup can be mixed with icing sugar for glazing nut-flavoured breads.

LEFT: The glossy top to Hot Cross Buns is achieved by glazing after baking with a mixture of milk and sugar.

POLISH BABKA

Vodka is the surprise ingredient in this classic Polish cake, made at Eastertime. The dough is enriched with eggs and flavoured with citrus peel and raisins.

60ml/4 tbsp vodka
2.5ml/½ tsp saffron threads
15ml/1 tbsp grated orange rind
15ml/1 tbsp grated lemon rind
115g/4oz/½ cup butter, softened
75g/3oz/6 tbsp caster (superfine) sugar
3 eggs
30ml/2 tbsp water
400g/14oz/3½ cups unbleached white bread flour
2.5ml/½ tsp salt
10ml/2 tsp easy-blend (rapid-rise) dried yeast
75g/3oz/½ cup raisins
75g/3oz/½ cup dried sour cherries
115g/4oz/1 cup icing (confectioners') sugar
15ml/1 tbsp lemon juice

FOR THE DECORATION
toasted flaked almonds
pared orange rind or candied orange peel

SERVES 8–10

1 Steep the vodka, saffron and citrus rinds together for 30 minutes. Beat the butter and sugar in a bowl until pale and creamy. Tip the saffron mixture into the bread pan, then add the eggs and water. If necessary, reverse the order in which you add the liquid and dry ingredients.

2 Add the flour, covering the liquid. Add the salt in a corner. Make an indent in the flour; add the yeast. Set to the dough setting; use basic raisin dough setting (if available). Press Start.

3 Mix for 5 minutes, then add the creamed butter and sugar mixture.

4 Tip in the raisins and dried sour cherries when the machine beeps, or 5 minutes before the end of the kneading cycle. Lightly oil a brioche tin. When the cycle has finished, remove the dough from the pan and place on a floured surface.

5 Knock back (punch down) gently, and shape into a plump round ball. Place in the prepared tin, cover with lightly oiled clear film (plastic wrap) and leave in a warm place for about 2 hours, or until it has risen almost to the top of the tin.

6 Preheat the oven to 200°C/400°F/Gas 6. Bake the babka for 20 minutes. Reduce the oven temperature to 190°C/375°F/Gas 5 and continue to bake for 15–20 minutes more, until golden.

7 Turn the babka out on to a wire rack to cool. Meanwhile, make the icing. Place the icing sugar in a small bowl and add the lemon juice and 15ml/1 tbsp hot water. Mix well, then drizzle the icing over the cake. Sprinkle over the almonds and pared orange rind or candied orange peel to decorate.

TOPPINGS

In addition to glazes, extra ingredients can be sprinkled over breads to give the finished loaf further interest. Toppings can alter the appearance, flavour and texture of the bread, so are an important part of any recipe. They also allow you to add your own individual stamp to a bread by using a topping of your own invention.

MACHINE-BAKED BREADS

A topping can be added at various stages: at the beginning of the baking cycle, about 10 minutes after baking begins, or immediately after baking while the bread is still hot. If you choose to add the topping at the beginning of baking, only open the lid for the shortest possible time, so heat loss is limited to the minimum. Before you add a topping, brush the bread with a glaze. This will ensure that the topping sticks to the loaf. Most machine breads are brushed with an egg, milk or water glaze.

If applying a topping to a bread after baking, remove the bread pan carefully from the machine and close the lid to retain the heat. Using oven gloves, quickly loosen the bread from the pan, then put it back in the pan again (this will make the

ABOVE: Flaked almonds have been sprinkled over the top of this Raspberry and Almond Teabread, giving a broad hint of its delicious flavour and adding extra crunch.

final removal easier) then brush the loaf with the glaze and sprinkle over the chosen topping. Return the bread in the pan to the bread machine for 3–4 minutes, which allows the glaze to bake on and secure the topping. With this method, the chosen topping will not cook and brown in the same way it would were it added at the beginning of baking.

When using grain as a topping, the general rule is to match it to the grain or flour used in the bread itself; for example, a bread containing millet flakes or millet seeds is often sprinkled with millet flour.

If a flavouring has been incorporated into the dough, you may be able to top the loaf with the same ingredient, to provide a hint of what is inside. Try sprinkling a little grated Parmesan on to a cheese loaf about 10 minutes after baking begins, or, for a loaf flavoured with herbs, add an appropriate dried herb as a topping immediately after baking.

LEFT: Rolled oats and wheat grain are sprinkled on to sweet potato bread just before it begins to bake to give the loaf a delightful rustic look.

MINI BRIOCHE

*Rich yet light, these buttery breads, with their characteristic fluted shape,
can be eaten with both sweet and savoury foods.*

30ml/2 tbsp milk
2 eggs
*225g/8oz/2 cups unbleached white
bread flour*
2.5ml/½ tsp salt
15ml/1 tbsp caster (superfine) sugar
50g/2oz butter, melted
*7.5ml/1½ tsp easy-blend (rapid-rise)
dried yeast*
1 egg yolk, to glaze
15ml/1 tbsp milk, to glaze

MAKES 12

COOK'S TIP

This is a rich dough and may need
more than the standard proving time.
If it has not risen very much by the
time the dough programme ends,
leave the dough in the machine for
another 30 minutes, turning off the
machine and leaving the lid shut.

1 Pour the milk and eggs into the bread
machine pan. If the instructions for your
bread machine specify that the yeast is
to be placed in the pan first, simply
reverse the order in which you add the
liquid and dry ingredients.

2 Sprinkle over the flour, ensuring that
it covers the liquid. Add the salt, sugar
and butter, placing them in separate
corners of the bread pan. Make a small
indent in the centre of the flour (but not
down as far as the liquid) and add the
easy-blend dried yeast.

3 Set the bread machine to the dough
setting; use basic dough setting (if
available). Press Start. Lightly oil
12 small brioche moulds.

4 When the dough cycle has finished,
remove from the machine and place on a
floured surface. Knock it back (punch it
down) gently. Slice off a quarter of the
dough, cover with oiled clear film
(plastic wrap) and set aside. Divide the
remaining dough into 12 pieces.

5 Knead each piece of dough into a
small round. Place each round in an
oiled mould. Divide the reserved piece
of dough into 12 and shape into small
pear shapes.

6 To shape each mini brioche, make a
small hole or cut a cross in the top of
each large piece of dough. Place the
pear-shaped pieces of dough on top,
narrow end down. Cover with lightly
oiled clear film and leave in a warm
place for 30–45 minutes, or until well
risen. Meanwhile preheat the oven to
220°C/425°F/Gas 7.

7 Make the glaze by mixing the egg yolk
and milk together. Brush the mixture
over each brioche. Bake for 15 minutes,
or until the brioche are golden and have
risen well. Transfer them to a wire rack
to cool. Serve warm or cold.

FLOUR

To create a farmhouse-style finish, brush the loaf with water or milk glaze just before baking and dust lightly with flour. Use white flour, or wholemeal (whole-wheat) or Granary for a more rustic finish.

SMALL SEEDS

Seeds can be used to add flavour and texture in addition to a decorative finish. Try sesame, poppy, aniseed, caraway or cumin seeds. If adding sesame seeds immediately after baking, lightly toast until golden before adding.

SALT

Brush the top of a white loaf with water or egg glaze and sprinkle with a coarse sea salt, to give an attractive and crunchy topping. Sea salt is best applied at the beginning of baking or 10 minutes into the baking cycle.

MAIZEMEAL OR POLENTA

Use maizemeal (cornmeal), polenta, semolina or other speciality flours as a finish for breads containing these flours, such as Courgette Country Grain Bread.

LARGE SEEDS

Gently press pumpkin or sunflower seeds on to the top of a freshly glazed loaf to give an attractive finish and a bonus crunch.

WHEAT AND OAT BRAN FLAKES

These add both texture and fibre to bread as well as visual appeal. Sprinkle them over the top of the loaf after glazing at the beginning of baking.

ROLLED OATS

These make a decorative finish for white breads and breads flavoured with oatmeal. Rolled oats are best added just before or at the very beginning of baking.

PEPPER AND PAPRIKA

Freshly ground black pepper and paprika both add spiciness to savoury breads. This tasty topping can be added before, during or after baking.

ICING SUGAR

Dust cooked sweet breads, teabreads or cakes with icing (confectioner's) sugar for a finished look. Add 2.5ml/½tsp spice before sprinkling for added flavour.

Hazelnut Twist Cake

Easy to make yet impressive, this sweet bread consists of layers of ground nuts, twisted through a rich dough, topped with a maple-flavoured icing.

230ml/8fl oz/1 cup water
1 egg
450g/1lb/4 cups unbleached white
bread flour
45ml/3 tbsp skimmed milk powder
(non fat dry milk)
grated rind of 1 orange
2.5ml/½ tsp salt
50g/2oz/¼ cup caster (superfine) sugar
75g/3oz/6 tbsp butter, melted
7.5ml/1½ tsp easy-blend (rapid-rise)
dried yeast
flaked (sliced) almonds or slivered
hazelnuts, to decorate

FOR THE FILLING
115g/4oz/1 cup ground hazelnuts
100g/3½oz/1 cup ground almonds
100g/3½oz/scant ½ cup light
muscovado (brown) sugar
2.5ml/½ tsp freshly grated nutmeg
2 egg whites
15ml/1 tbsp brandy

FOR THE TOPPING
60ml/4 tbsp icing
(confectioners') sugar
15ml/1 tbsp hot water
30ml/2 tbsp natural maple syrup

SERVES 6–8

1 Pour the water and egg into the bread pan. Reverse the order in which you add the wet and dry ingredients if necessary. Sprinkle over the flour, covering the liquid. Add the milk powder and orange rind. Place the salt, sugar and butter in separate corners. Make a shallow indent in the centre of the flour; add the yeast.

2 Set the bread machine to the dough setting; use basic dough setting (if available). Press Start. Lightly oil a 23cm/9in springform ring cake tin (pan).

3 When the dough cycle has finished, place the dough on a lightly floured surface. Knock it back (punch it down) gently, then roll it out to a 65 × 45cm/26 × 18in rectangle. Cut the dough in half lengthways.

4 Make the filling by mixing all of the ingredients in a bowl. Divide the filling in half. Spread one portion over each piece of dough, leaving a 1cm/½in clear border along one long edge of each piece.

5 Starting from the other long edge, roll up each piece of dough, Swiss (jelly) roll fashion. Place the two pieces next to each other and twist them together.

6 Brush the ends of the dough rope with a little water. Loop the rope in the prepared springform tin and gently press the ends together to seal.

7 Cover the tin with lightly oiled clear film (plastic wrap) and then leave the dough in a warm place for 30–45 minutes, or until it has risen and is puffy. Preheat the oven to 200°C/400°F/Gas 6.

8 Bake for 30–35 minutes, or until golden and well risen. Leave to cool slightly, then turn out on to a wire rack.

9 Make the icing by mixing the icing sugar, hot water and maple syrup in a bowl. Drizzle over the warm cake. Sprinkle with a few flaked almonds or slivered hazelnuts and leave to cool completely before serving.

HAND-SHAPED BREAD

All of the toppings used on machine-baked breads can also be added to breads that are hand-shaped and baked in an oven. There are several methods that can be used for adding a topping to hand-shaped rolls and breads.

SPRINKLING WITH FLOUR

If you are using flour, this should be sprinkled over the dough immediately after shaping and again before slashing and baking, to give a rustic finish. Match the flour to the type of bread being made. Unbleached white bread flour is ideal for giving soft rolls and breads a fine finish. Use maizemeal (cornmeal), ground rice or rice flour for crumpets and muffins and brown and Granary flours on wholegrain (whole-meal) breads.

GROUND RICE OR RICE FLOUR

Muffins are enhanced with a ground rice or rice flour topping.

WHOLEMEAL FLOUR

Wholemeal flour toppings complement wholegrain dough whether made into loaves or rolls.

ABOVE: An Easter tea ring is glazed with an icing made from icing sugar and orange juice, then sprinkled with pecan nuts and candied orange.

ROLLING DOUGH IN SEEDS

Sprinkle seeds, salt or any other fine topping on a work surface, then roll the shaped but unproved dough in the chosen topping until it is evenly coated. This is ideal for coating wholegrain breads with pumpkin seeds or wheat flakes. After rolling, place the dough on the sheet for its final rising.

SESAME SEEDS

Dough sticks can be rolled in small seeds for a delicious crunchy topping.

MIXED PEEL BRAID

A succulent citrus filling with a hint of ginger provides the pleasant surprise in this attractively braided coffee-time cake.

90ml/6 tbsp milk
1 egg
280g/10oz/2½ cups unbleached white bread flour
5ml/1 tsp mixed (apple pie) spice
2.5ml/½ tsp salt
25g/1oz/2 tbsp caster (superfine) sugar
50g/2oz/¼ cup butter, melted
5ml/1 tsp easy-blend (rapid-rise) dried yeast
115g/4oz/⅔ cup mixed (candied) peel
50g/2oz/⅓ cup sultanas (golden raisins)
25g/1oz/¼ cup walnut pieces, chopped
25g/1oz/2 tbsp chopped glacé (candied) ginger
45ml/3 tbsp three fruit marmalade

FOR THE GLAZE
1 egg yolk
15ml/1 tbsp caster (superfine) sugar
15ml/1 tbsp milk

SERVES 8

1 Pour the milk and egg into the bread machine pan. If necessary for your bread machine, reverse the order of adding the wet and dry ingredients.

2 Sprinkle over the flour to cover the liquid. Add the mixed spice. Put the salt, sugar and butter in separate corners. Make a small indent in the centre of the flour and add the yeast.

3 Set the bread machine to the dough setting; use basic dough setting (if available). Press Start. Lightly oil a baking sheet.

4 When the dough cycle has finished, remove the dough from the machine and place it on a lightly floured surface. Knock it back (punch it down) gently, then roll it out to a 28 × 40cm/11 × 16in rectangle.

5 Make the filling by combining the mixed peel, sultanas, walnuts, ginger and marmalade in a bowl. Spread the mixture lengthways over the middle third of the rolled-out dough, leaving a 2.5cm/1in border at either end. Using a sharp knife, cut the two strips of dough either side of the filling into diagonal strips angled towards you, 2cm/¾in wide.

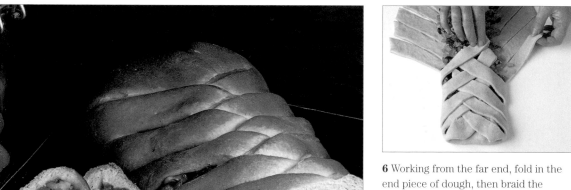

6 Working from the far end, fold in the end piece of dough, then braid the dough strips over the filling. Tuck in the end to seal. Place the braid on the baking sheet. Cover it with lightly oiled clear film (plastic wrap) and leave in a warm place for 30–45 minutes to rise.

7 Meanwhile, preheat the oven to 200°C/400°F/Gas 6. Make the glaze by mixing the egg yolk, sugar and milk in a bowl. Brush the mixture over the braid. Bake for 10 minutes, then reduce the oven temperature to 190°C/375°F/Gas 5 and bake for 10–15 minutes more, or until the braid is golden and well risen. Turn out on to a wire rack to cool.

Sweet Breads & Yeast Cakes

ADDING A TOPPING AFTER A GLAZE

Some toppings are sprinkled over the bread after glazing and immediately before baking. In addition to the toppings suggested for machine-baked breads, these toppings can be used:

CANDIED FRUITS

Whole or chopped candied fruits make an attractive topping for festive breads and buns. Add the fruits after an egg glaze. Candied fruits can also be used after baking, with a jam or icing sugar glaze to stick the fruits to the bread.

NUTS

Just before baking, brush sweet or savoury breads and rolls with glaze and sprinkle with chopped or flaked (sliced) almonds, chopped cashews, chopped or whole walnuts or pecan nuts.

SMALL SEEDS AND GRAINS

Seeds and grains such as millet grain, black onion seeds and mustard seeds all add texture and taste to breads. Try them as a topping for loaves and flatbreads such as lavash and naan.

VEGETABLES

Brush savoury breads and rolls with an egg glaze or olive oil and then sprinkle with finely chopped raw onion, raw peppers, sun-dried tomatoes or olives for an extremely tasty crust.

CHEESE

Grated cheeses, such as Parmesan, Cheddar or Pecorino, are best for sprinkling on to dough just before baking, resulting in a chewy, flavoursome crust.

FRESH HERBS

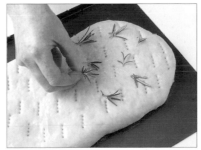

Use fresh herbs, such as rosemary, thyme, sage or basil for Italian-style flatbreads. Chopped herbs also make a good topping for rolls.

USING SUGAR AS A TOPPING

Sugar is available in many forms, so chose one appropriate for your topping.

DEMERARA SUGAR

Before baking, brush unbaked buns and cakes with butter or milk and sprinkle with demerara (raw) sugar for a crunchy finish.

SUGAR COATING

Yeast doughs that are deep-fried, such as doughnuts and Saffron Plaits can be sprinkled or tossed in a sugar coating. Toss doughnuts in caster sugar that has been mixed with a little ground cinnamon or freshly grated nutmeg, or flavoured using a vanilla pod (bean).

DUSTING WITH ICING SUGAR

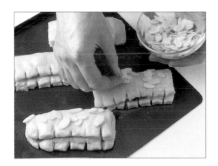

Use a fine sieve to sprinkle cooked buns and yeast cakes, such as Devonshire Splits, with icing (confectioner's) sugar. Large cakes and breads such as Spiced Fruit Kugelhopf will also benefit from a light dusting of icing sugar, as do fruit-filled Savarins. If serving a bread or cake warm, dust with icing sugar when ready to serve to avoid the topping soaking into the bread.

PEACH BRANDY BABAS

*These light, delicate sponges are moistened with a syrup flavoured with
peach brandy before being filled with whipped cream and fruit. You can vary
the flavour of the syrup by using orange or coconut liqueur or dark rum.*

1 Pour the milk and eggs into the bread pan. If the instructions for your machine specify that the yeast is to be placed in the pan first, reverse the order in which you add the liquid and dry ingredients to the pan.

2 Sprinkle over the flour, ensuring that it covers the liquid. Add the cinnamon, then place the salt and sugar in separate corners. Make a small indent in the centre of the flour (but not down as far as the liquid) and add the yeast.

3 Set the bread machine to the dough setting; use basic dough setting (if available). Press Start. Lightly oil eight small savarin tins, each with a diameter of 10cm/4in.

4 When the machine has finished mixing the dough, let the dough cycle continue for a further 15 minutes, then stop the machine and scrape the dough into a large measuring jug (cup). Gradually beat in the melted butter.

5 Pour the batter into the prepared tins, half filling them. Cover with lightly oiled clear film (plastic wrap) and leave in a warm place until the batter reaches the tin tops.

6 Meanwhile, preheat the oven to 190°C/375°F/Gas 5. Bake for 20 minutes, or until golden and well risen. Turn out on to a wire rack to cool. Slide a large tray under the rack.

7 To make the syrup for the babas, place the granulated sugar and water in a small pan and heat gently, stirring occasionally, until the sugar has dissolved. Bring to the boil and boil hard for 2 minutes without stirring. Remove the syrup from the heat and stir in the peach brandy. Spoon the syrup over the babas. Then scrape up any syrup which has dripped on to the tray with a spatula and repeat the process until all the syrup is absorbed.

8 When the babas are cold, whip the cream, sugar and vanilla essence in a bowl until the cream just forms soft peaks. Fill the babas with the flavoured cream and decorate them with the fresh fruits of your choice.

*100ml/3½fl oz/7 tbsp milk
4 eggs
225g/8oz/2 cups unbleached white
bread flour
5ml/1 tsp ground cinnamon
2.5ml/½ tsp salt
25g/1oz/2 tbsp caster (superfine) sugar
5ml/1 tsp easy-blend (rapid-rise)
dried yeast
100g/3½oz/7 tbsp butter, melted
115g/4oz/½ cup granulated sugar
150ml/5fl oz/⅔ cup water
90ml/6 tbsp peach brandy*

*FOR THE DECORATION
150ml/5fl oz/⅔ cup double
(heavy) cream
15ml/1 tbsp caster (superfine) sugar
3–4 drops natural vanilla
essence (extract)
fresh fruits, to decorate*

MAKES 8

USING SOURDOUGHS AND STARTERS

For bread to rise, some sort of raising agent or leaven – must be used. In most cases, this will be yeast, or perhaps bicarbonate of soda, but it is also possible to initiate the fermentation process naturally, by the action of wild yeasts, present in the air, on a medium such as flour or potatoes. When this is done, the mixture that results is called a starter.

There are two basic starters: a natural leaven and a yeasted starter. The former uses only airborne yeast spores, which create a lactic fermentation, as when milk turns sour. A yeasted starter includes a small amount of baker's yeast to kick-start the fermentation and develop a desired strain of yeast.

Sourdoughs are made using starters which develop over several days to produce a distinctive tanginess or "soured" flavour. Depending on how starters are made, how long they are left to ferment and how they are used, different flavours as well as textures can be achieved. Many of the Continental breads owe their flavours and textures to starters, which also influence their keeping qualities.

BREADMAKING METHODS

There are three basic methods of making breads: the direct method, the sourdough method, and the sponge method.

In the direct method, the flour, water and yeast are mixed, and once the dough has risen, the bread is baked in the shortest possible time. This is the conventional way of bread making.

The sourdough method is a much lengthier process. First, a starter must be made – this takes several days – and then this must be mixed with additional flour and other ingredients, often in several stages, called "refreshments", a process that takes at least 24 hours.

The sponge method is a compromise between the previous two. The dough is made using baker's yeast. A portion of the dough is mixed and allowed to ferment before the remaining ingredients are added. The process enhances the flavour and texture of the finished bread.

THE SOURDOUGH METHOD

Sourdough breads can be made from either a natural leaven or a yeasted starter. Most natural sourdough cultures can be turned into a starter within about 5 days. Flour and water are the basic ingredients, but other ingredients may be added to encourage the fermentation, such as honey, malt extract, soured milk, ground cumin or even a little baker's yeast.

The French term for this flour and water mixture is a "chef". The chef is left to ferment for 2–3 days, which brings about a lactic acid action, giving rise to the basic sour flavour. Once this dough is aerated and slightly sour, it is mixed or "refreshed" with more flour and water, to feed the fermentation process. After another 24 hours or so it is refreshed again, and becomes a natural leavener, or levain. This is left to ferment for about 8 hours more, when it is ready for use in the final bread dough.

Bread made by this method will taste slightly sour and will have a dense moist crumb, chewy crust and extremely good keeping qualities. Sourdough starters have varying textures, so do not worry if you come across different consistencies. Often American starters tend to be less stiff.

THE FRENCH SPONGE METHOD

The French sponge or poolish is made with yeast and some of the flour and water from the bread recipe, but no salt to retard the fermentation. The poolish is usually fermented for a minimum of 2 hours, and for up to 8 hours. Usually less yeast is used than with the direct method so the dough rises more slowly, giving it time to ripen and develop a springy texture. It combines the chewiness of a sourdough with the lightness of a basic bread.

The wetter the mix, the quicker it will rise, as the flour and water will provide less resistance for the yeast.

THE ITALIAN SPONGE METHOD

The Italian sponge or biga takes at least 12 hours, often longer, to ripen, allowing time for the dough to develop and rise to three times its original bulk before collapsing. The longer it is left the more developed the flavour will be. These breads have an open, holey, slightly moist and chewy texture. Their flavour and aroma tend to be yeasty and champagne-like. Ciabatta is a perfect example.

MAKING AN ITALIAN SPONGE

1 The flour, water and yeast for the biga are added to the bread machine and mixed as usual.

2 It is allowed to rise for several hours until it has tripled in size. After 12 hours it should be starting to collapse.

3 When the dough collapses, it is ready to be combined with the remaining ingredients for the bread.

Strawberry Chocolate Savarin

100ml/3½fl oz/7 tbsp milk
4 eggs
225g/8oz/2 cups unbleached white
bread flour
40g/1½oz/3 tbsp cocoa powder
(unsweetened)
2.5ml/½ tsp salt
25g/1oz/2 tbsp caster (superfine) sugar
100g/3½oz/7 tbsp butter, melted
5ml/1 tsp easy-blend (rapid-rise)
dried yeast
115g/4oz/½ cup granulated sugar
75ml/2½fl oz/scant ⅓ cup white wine
45ml/3 tbsp brandy
physalis and strawberry leaves,
to decorate

For the Filling
150ml/5fl oz/⅔ cup double (heavy)
cream, whipped, or crème fraîche
225g/8oz/2 cups strawberries, halved
115g/4oz/1 cup raspberries

Serves 6–8

VARIATION
The savarin can be filled with other
fruits, such as grapes, raspberries,
currants, peaches or blackberries.
Alternatively, fill with chantilly cream,
(slightly sweetened, vanilla flavoured
whipped cream) and sprinkle
chopped nuts over the top.

*This light spongy cake is soaked in a wine and brandy syrup before being
filled with succulent fresh strawberries to make an exquisite dessert.*

1 Pour the milk and eggs into the bread
pan. If your machine specifies that the
yeast is to be placed in the pan first,
reverse the order in which you add the
liquid and dry ingredients.

2 Sift the flour and cocoa powder
together. Sprinkle the mixture over the
liquid in the pan, covering it completely.
Place the salt, sugar and butter in
separate corners. Make a shallow indent
in the centre of the flour; add the yeast.

3 Set the machine to the dough setting;
use basic dough setting (if available).
Press Start. Lightly oil a 1.5 litre/2½ pint/
6¼ cup savarin or ring mould.

4 When the machine has finished mixing
the ingredients, leave it on the dough
setting for 20 minutes then stop the
machine. Pour the dough mixture into
the mould, cover with oiled clear film
(plastic wrap) and leave in a warm place
for 45–60 minutes, or until the dough
almost reaches the top of the tin.

5 Meanwhile, preheat the oven to 200°C/
400°F/Gas 6. Bake for 25–30 minutes,
or until the savarin is golden and well
risen. Turn out on to a wire rack to cool,
with a plate beneath the rack.

6 Make the syrup. Place the sugar, wine
and 75ml/2½fl oz/⅓ cup water in a pan.
Heat gently, stirring until the sugar
dissolves. Bring to the boil then lower the
heat and simmer for 2 minutes. Remove
from the heat and stir in the brandy.

7 Spoon the syrup over the savarin.
Repeat with any syrup which has
collected on the plate. Transfer to a
serving plate and leave to cool. To serve,
fill the centre with the cream or crème
fraîche and top with the strawberries
and raspberries. Decorate with physalis
and strawberry leaves.

THE OLD DOUGH METHOD

A variation of the direct method, this approach is exactly what its name suggests. A small piece of dough is removed from a batch of risen dough and set aside for adding to the dough for the next loaf of bread. This is a quick and easy alternative to making a starter and will add texture and improve the taste of the bread to which it is added.

The old dough method is perfect for the bread machine. Make a batch of dough using the regular dough cycle. When the bread is ready for shaping, pull off about 115g/4oz of the dough, place it in a bowl and cover with clear film (plastic wrap). If using within 4 hours leave at room temperature; if not, put the bowl in the refrigerator, but let the dough return to room temperature before use. It can be kneaded into a batch of dough which will be shaped by hand or added with the ingredients for a machine-baked bread.

If you are adding old dough to a loaf which is to be baked in a machine, reduce the flour and liquid slightly when you make up the new batch of dough. The following recipe is suitable for a medium or large machine. If you have a smaller machine reduce the quantities by a quarter. You can increase the quantities by a quarter for a large machine if you like.

ABOVE: San Francisco-style Sourdough is made from airborne spores of yeast, and has no baker's yeast added to it. The variety of yeast strains in the atmosphere will mean that the bread tastes slightly different from place to place.

USING THE OLD DOUGH METHOD

1 Tear about 115g/4oz dough off bread that is ready for shaping. Place in a bowl and cover with clear film (plastic wrap). Set aside at room temperature or, if not using within 4 hours, in the refrigerator. Return to room temperature before use.

2 Pour 280ml/10fl oz/1¼ cups water into the bread machine pan. Add the old dough which has been reserved. However, if the instructions for your machine specify that the dry ingredients are to be placed in the bread pan first, reverse the order in which you add the dry ingredients and the water and reserved dough.

3 Sprinkle over 450g/1lb/4 cups unbleached white bread flour. Add 7.5ml/1½ tsp salt, 15ml/1 tbsp granulated sugar and 25g/1oz butter, placing these ingredients in separate corners of the bread pan.

4 Make a small indent in the centre of the flour and add 5ml/1 tsp easy-blend dried yeast.

5 Set the bread machine to the basic/normal setting, medium crust. Press Start. At the end of the baking cycle, remove the bread from the pan and turn out on to a wire rack to cool.

BAVARIAN PLUM CAKE

*As this bakes, the juices from the plums trickle through to the base, making a
deliciously succulent, fruity cake. Serve it with coffee or as a dessert with
crème fraîche or ice cream.*

90ml/6 tbsp milk
1 egg
*225g/8oz/2 cups unbleached white
bread flour*
5ml/1 tsp ground cinnamon
2.5ml/½ tsp salt
40g/1½oz/3 tbsp caster (superfine) sugar
25g/1oz/2 tbsp butter, melted
*5ml/1 tsp easy-blend (rapid-rise)
dried yeast*
675g/1½lb plums
icing (confectioners') sugar, for dusting

SERVES 8

3 Make a small indent in the centre of
the flour (but not down as far as the
liquid) and add the yeast.

4 Set the bread machine to the dough
setting; use basic dough setting (if
available). Press Start. Lightly oil a
27 × 18cm/10½ × 7in rectangular baking
tin (pan) that is about 4cm/1½in deep.

5 When the dough cycle has finished,
remove the dough and place it on a
lightly floured surface. Knock it back
(punch it down) gently, then roll it out
to fit the tin. Ease it into position.

1 Pour the milk into the bread machine
pan and add the egg. If the instructions
for your machine specify that the yeast
is to be placed in the pan first, simply
reverse the order in which you add the
liquid and dry ingredients.

VARIATION
Replace the plums with apple wedges
or nectarine slices. Use dessert apples
as cooking apples will be too tart.
Allow four to five depending on their
size. Sprinkle the top with demerara
(raw) sugar 5 minutes before the end
of baking, and return to the oven.

2 Sprinkle over the flour, ensuring that
it covers the milk and egg completely.
Add the ground cinnamon. Place the
salt, sugar and butter in separate
corners of the bread pan.

6 Cut the plums into quarters and
remove the stones (pits). Arrange on
the dough, so that they overlap slightly.
Cover with lightly oiled clear film
(plastic wrap) and leave in a warm place
for 30–45 minutes, to rise. Meanwhile,
preheat the oven to 190°C/375°F/Gas 5.

7 Bake the cake for 30–35 minutes, or
until golden and well risen. Dust with
icing sugar and serve warm.

MAKING A YOGURT STARTER

Variations on the basic flour and water starter can be made to add complexity and uniqueness to the flavour and texture of bread. This yogurt starter will give a flavour similar to that of San Francisco-style Sourdough because the lactose in the milk products sours in a similar way.

1 Place 75ml/5 tbsp natural (plain) yogurt in a bowl. Pour 175ml/6fl oz/¾ cup skimmed milk into a pan and heat gently.

2 Stir the milk into the yogurt. Cover with clear film and leave in a warm place for 8–24 hours, or until thickened. Stir in any clear liquid which may have separated and risen to the surface.

REPLENISHING A STARTER

After first making the starter, use or replenish within 3–4 days. When half has been used, replenish with 50g/2oz/½ cup white bread flour and 45ml/3 tbsp skimmed milk and 15ml/1 tbsp natural (plain) yogurt or 60ml/4 tbsp skimmed milk. If used daily, keep the starter at room temperature. If not, store in the refrigerator; bring back to room temperature before use.

3 Gradually mix in 115g/4oz/1 cup organic white bread flour, stirring to incorporate evenly.

BELOW: French Couronne is made using a chef starter which becomes a levain, a natural leavener.

4 Cover and leave in a warm place for 2–3 days, until the mixture is full of bubbles and smells pleasantly sour. (Uncover to check the aroma of the starter.) Use instead of the usual starter for San Francisco-style Sourdough or incorporate into a basic bread recipe.

Using Sourdoughs and Starters

PEACH STREUSELKUCHEN

100ml/3½fl oz/7 tbsp milk
1 egg
250g/9oz/2¼ cups unbleached white
bread flour
2.5ml/½ tsp salt
40g/1½oz/3 tbsp caster (superfine) sugar
25g/1oz/2 tbsp butter, melted
5ml/1 tsp easy-blend (rapid-rise)
dried yeast
4 peaches, halved and stoned (pitted)

FOR THE TOPPING
75g/3oz/¾ cup plain (all-purpose) flour
40g/1½oz/⅓ cup ground almonds
50g/2oz/¼ cup butter, diced and
softened
40g/1½oz/4 tbsp caster sugar
5ml/1 tsp ground cinnamon

SERVES 8

This peach-filled German yeast cake is finished with a crunchy almond and cinnamon topping which is quite irresistible.

1 Pour the milk and egg into the bread pan. If the instructions for your bread machine specify that the yeast should go in first, reverse the order of wet and dry ingredients.

2 Sprinkle over the flour, ensuring that it covers the milk and egg completely. Then add the salt, sugar and butter, placing them in three separate corners of the bread pan. Make a small indent in the centre of the flour (but not down as far as the liquid) and add the easy-blend dried yeast.

3 Set the bread machine to the dough setting; use basic dough setting (if available). Press Start. Lightly oil a 25cm/10in springform cake tin (pan).

4 When the dough cycle has finished, remove the dough from the pan and place it on a lightly floured surface. Knock it back (punch it down) gently, then roll it out to fit the tin. Ease it into position.

5 Slice the peaches thickly and arrange them on top of the dough. Next, make the topping. Rub the flour, ground almonds and butter together until the mixture resembles coarse breadcrumbs. Stir in the caster sugar and cinnamon. Sprinkle the topping over the peaches.

6 Cover the dough with lightly oiled clear film (plastic wrap) and leave in a warm place for about 20–25 minutes, to rise slightly. Meanwhile, preheat the oven to 190°C/375°F/Gas 5.

7 Bake the cake for 25–30 minutes, or until evenly golden. Leave it to cool in the tin for a few minutes and serve warm, or turn out on to a wire rack to allow to cool completely.

2 Stir the starter and use the amount required in the recipe. If your purpose in bringing the starter to room temperature is just so that you can feed it, pour half of the starter into a measuring jug, note the volume, then throw it away. This is so you will know how much to replenish.

3 Replenish the starter by adding flour and water (in equal parts by volume). Use organic white or wholemeal (wholewheat) bread flour, or a combination of both. Wholemeal flour develops a more intense sour flavour. Add a quantity that equates to the amount of starter that has been removed. Mix until smooth.

USING A STARTER IN YOUR BREAD MACHINE

You can try adding a sourdough starter to one of your favourite recipes for a more complex flavour. Add it to a basic white, wholemeal (whole-wheat), mixed grain or rye bread. Here are a few pointers:

• Always bring the starter back to room temperature before using if it has been stored in the refrigerator.

• If your starter was made from a mixture of roughly half flour and half liquid, when you add it to the recipe, reduce the liquid in the recipe by the quantity of liquid in the starter, that is by half the total volume of the starter.

• The starter can be used in two ways. Try it in doughs that are made in the bread machine but shaped by hand and baked in the oven, or use it in a dough that is made and baked in the machine. If the latter, check the dough during the rising stage to make sure it is not rising too high; you can always override the programme and set the machine to the bake only programme.

• If the dough hasn't risen as much as you would like, you will need to bake it in the oven. Remove the dough from the bread machine and shape it by hand. Leave to rise until it has almost doubled in size, then bake in the normal way.

ABOVE : Ciabatta is made using the Italian sponge method.

REFRESHING A SOURDOUGH STARTER

Each time you use a sourdough starter, it needs to be replenished. Also, if you are not likely to be using it for some time, it is important to "feed" the starter regularly, with flour and liquid, to keep it active. The amount of flour and water you add to the starter to replenish it should equate to what was removed, either to be used in dough or discarded.

Once established, a sourdough starter can be kept in the fridge almost indefinitely. In fact, the flavour of the sourdough starter gets better with age. If your starter begins to turn pink or develops a mould, however, discard it and start again.

1 Remove the starter from the fridge. It should be at room temperature before it's added to a recipe or fed to keep it active.

4 Cover and leave in a warm place for a few hours until it starts to bubble and ferment. Place in the fridge until needed.

MANGO AND BANANA BREAD

Tropical fruit juice, fresh banana and dried mango give this light-textured loaf its Caribbean flavour.

1 Pour the fruit juice and buttermilk into the bread machine pan. Add the mashed banana(s) to the bread pan, with the honey. If necessary for your machine, reverse the order in which you add the liquid and dry ingredients.

2 Sprinkle over the flour, ensuring that it covers the liquid. Place the salt and butter in separate corners of the bread pan. Make a shallow indent in the centre of the flour and add the yeast.

3 Set the bread machine to the basic/normal setting, with raisin setting (if available), medium crust. Press Start.

4 Add the chopped mango pieces when the machine beeps to add extra ingredients, or 5 minutes before the end of the kneading cycle.

5 Remove the bread from the pan at the end of the baking cycle and turn out on to a wire rack to cool.

SMALL

30ml/2 tbsp orange and mango juice
150ml/generous 5fl oz/scant ⅔ cup buttermilk
150g/5oz/1 medium banana, peeled and mashed
30ml/2 tbsp clear honey
350g/12oz/3 cups unbleached white bread flour
5ml/1 tsp salt
25g/1oz/2 tbsp butter
5ml/1 tsp easy-blend (rapid-rise) dried yeast
25g/1oz/¼ cup dried mango, chopped

MEDIUM

60ml/2fl oz/¼ cup orange and mango juice
200ml/7fl oz/⅞ cup buttermilk
175g/6oz/1 large banana, peeled and mashed
45ml/3 tbsp clear honey
500g/1lb 2oz/4½ cups unbleached white bread flour
5ml/1 tsp salt
40g/1½oz/3 tbsp butter
5ml/1 tsp easy-blend dried yeast
40g/1½oz/⅛ cup dried mango, chopped

LARGE

60ml/2fl oz/¼ cup orange and mango juice
260ml/9fl oz/1⅛ cups buttermilk
300g/10½oz/2 medium bananas, peeled and mashed
60ml/4 tbsp clear honey
675g/1½lb/6 cups unbleached white bread flour
7.5ml/1½ tsp salt
50g/2oz/¼ cup butter
7.5ml/1½ tsp easy-blend dried yeast
50g/2oz/½ cup dried mango, chopped

MAKES 1 LOAF

COOK'S TIP
Select ripe bananas if you can for this recipe, as they are softer and easier to mash.

Even the most comprehensive bread-machine manual cannot possibly cover all the hints and tips you will need. As you gain experience and confidence you will be able to solve more and more of any little problems that crop up. Here are a few pointers to help you along the road to successful baking.

TEMPERATURE AND HUMIDITY

The bread machine is not a sealed environment, and temperature and humidity can affect the finished results. On dry days, dry ingredients contain less water and on humid days they hold more.

The temperature of the ingredients is a very important factor in determining the success of machine baked bread. Some machines specify that all ingredients should be at room temperature; others state that ingredients can be added from the fridge. Some machines have pre-heating cycles to bring the ingredients to an optimum temperature of around 20–25°C/68–77°F, before mixing starts. It is recommended that you use ingredients at room temperature. Water can be used straight from the cold tap. Lukewarm water may be beneficial for the rapid bake cycle on cold days.

Hot weather can mean that doughs will rise faster, so on very hot days start with chilled ingredients, using milk or eggs straight from the refrigerator.

Icy winter weather and cold draughts will inhibit the action of the yeast, so either move your machine to a warmer spot, or warm liquids before adding them to the bread pan. On very cold days, let the water stand at room temperature for about half an hour before adding the other ingredients to the pan, or add a little warm water to bring it up to a temperature of around 20°C/68°F, but no hotter.

QUALITY PRODUCE

Use only really fresh, good quality ingredients. The bread machine can not improve poor quality produce. Make sure the yeast is within its use-by date. Yeast beyond its expiry date will produce poor results.

MEASURING INGREDIENTS

Measure both the liquids and the dry ingredients carefully. Most problems occur when ingredients are inaccurately measured, when one ingredient is forgotten or when the same ingredient is added twice. Do not mix imperial and metric measurements, as they are not interchangeable; stick to one set for the whole recipe.

Do not exceed the quantities of flour and liquid recommended for your machine. Mixing the extra ingredients may overload the motor and if you have too much dough it is likely to rise over the top of the pan.

FOLLOW THE INSTRUCTIONS

Always add the ingredients in the order suggested by the manufacturer. Whatever the order, keep the yeast dry and separate from any liquids added to the bread pan.

ADDING INGREDIENTS

Cut butter into pieces, especially if it is fairly firm, and/or when larger amounts than usual are required in the recipe. If a recipe requires ingredients such as cooked vegetables or fruit or toasted nuts to be added, leave them to cool to room temperature before adding them.

USING THE DELAY TIMER

Perishable ingredients such as eggs, fresh milk, cheese, meat, fruit and vegetables may deteriorate, especially in warm conditions, and could present a health risk. They should only be used in breads that are made immediately. Only use the delay timer for bread doughs that contain non-perishable ingredients.

CLEANING YOUR MACHINE

Unplug the machine before starting to clean it. Wipe down the outside regularly using a mild washing-up liquid and a damp, soft cloth. Avoid all abrasive cleansers and materials, even those that are designated for use on non-stick items, and do not use alcohol-based cleansers.

BREAD PAN AND KNEADING BLADE

Clean the bread pan and blade after each use. These parts should not be washed in the dishwasher as this might affect the non-stick surface and damage the packing around the shaft. Avoid immersing the bread pan in water. If you have difficulty extracting the blade from the pan, fill the base of the pan with lukewarm water and leave it to soak for a few minutes. Remove the blade and wipe it with a damp cloth. Wash the bread pan with mild washing-up liquid then rinse thoroughly. Always store the bread machine with the kneading blade removed from the shaft. The bread machine and components must be completely dry before putting away.

RUM AND RAISIN LOAF

Juicy raisins, plumped up with dark rum, flavour this tea-time loaf. It's more than good enough to serve just as it is, but slices can also be lightly toasted and buttered to ring the changes.

SMALL
75g/3oz/generous ½ cup raisins
22ml/1½ tbsp dark rum
1 egg
140ml/5fl oz/⅝ cup milk
350g/12oz/3 cups unbleached white
bread flour
1.5ml/¼ tsp ground ginger
25g/1oz/2 tbsp caster (superfine) sugar
2.5ml/½ tsp salt
40g/1½oz/3 tbsp butter
5ml/1 tsp easy-blend (rapid-rise)
dried yeast
10ml/2 tsp clear honey, warmed

MEDIUM
90g/3¼oz/⅔ cup raisins
30ml/2 tbsp dark rum
1 egg
240ml/8½fl oz/generous 1 cup milk
500g/1lb 2oz/4½ cups unbleached
white bread flour
2.5ml/½ tsp ground ginger
40g/1½oz/3 tbsp caster sugar
3.5ml/¾ tsp salt
50g/2oz/¼ cup butter
7.5ml/1½ tsp easy-blend dried yeast
15ml/1 tbsp clear honey, warmed

LARGE
115g/4oz/⅘ cup raisins
45ml/3 tbsp dark rum
2 eggs, lightly beaten
290ml/½pint/1¼ cups milk
675g/1½lb/6 cups unbleached white
bread flour
5ml/1 tsp ground ginger
50g/2oz/¼ cup caster sugar
5ml/1 tsp salt
65g/2½oz/5 tbsp butter
7.5ml/1½ tsp easy-blend dried yeast
15ml/1 tbsp clear honey, warmed

MAKES 1 LOAF

1 Place the raisins and rum in a small bowl and leave to soak for 2 hours, or longer if you can. Add the egg(s) and milk to the bread machine pan. If necessary for your machine, reverse the order in which you add the liquid and dry ingredients.

2 Sprinkle over the flour, ensuring that it covers the liquid completely. Add the ground ginger. Add the caster sugar, salt and butter, placing them in separate corners of the bread machine pan. Make a small indent in the centre of the flour (but not down as far as the liquid) and pour in the dried yeast.

3 Set the bread machine to the basic/normal setting, with raisin setting (if available), medium crust. Press Start. Add the raisins when the machine beeps to add extra ingredients, or after the first kneading.

4 Remove the bread at the end of the baking cycle and turn out on to a wire rack. Brush the top with honey and leave the loaf to cool.

ABOVE: A Granary loaf should be baked on the whole wheat setting, which has a longer rising cycle.

SPECIAL CONSIDERATIONS

Breads made with whole grains and heavier flours such as wholemeal (wholewheat), oatmeal or rye, or with added ingredients such as dried fruits and nuts, may rise more slowly than basic white loaves and be less tall. The same applies to breads with a lot of fat or egg. Breads with cheese, eggs or a high proportion of fats and/or sugar are more susceptible to burning. To avoid over-cooked crusts, select a light bake crust setting.

WATCHING THE DOUGH

Keep a flexible rubber spatula next to the machine and, if necessary, scrape down the sides of the pan after 5–10 minutes of the initial mixing cycle. The kneading blade sometimes fails to pick up a thick or sticky dough from the corners of the pan.

COOLING THE BREAD

It is best to remove the loaf from the pan as soon as the baking cycle finishes, or it may become slightly damp, even with a "stay warm" programme.

CHECKING THE DOUGH

Check the dough within the first 5 minutes of mixing, especially when you are trying a recipe for the first time. If the dough seems too wet and, instead of forming a ball, sticks to the sides of the pan, add a little flour, a spoonful at a time. However, the bread machine requires a dough that is slightly wetter than if you were mixing it by hand. If the dough is crumbly and won't form a ball, add liquid, one spoonful at a time. You will soon get used to the sound of the motor and notice if it is labouring due to a stiff mix. It is also worth checking the dough just before baking, to make sure it isn't about to rise over the top of the bread machine pan.

ABOVE: Dough is too wet and requires more flour.

ABOVE: Dough is too dry and requires more water.

SAFETY

1 Read the manufacturer's advice and instructions before operating your machine. Keep any instruction manuals provided with your machine handy for future reference.
2 If you touch the machine while it is in operation, be careful. The outside walls become hot when it is in baking mode.
3 Position the machine on a firm, level, heat-resistant surface, away from any other heat source.
4 Do not stand the bread machine in direct sunlight and allow at least 5–7.5cm/2–3in clearance on all sides when not in use.
5 Do not place anything on top of the machine lid.
6 Do not use the machine outdoors.
7 Do not immerse the machine, cable or plug in water and avoid using it near a source of water.
8 Be careful to keep your fingers away from the blade while the machine is kneading the dough, and never reach inside the machine during the baking cycle.
9 Keep the machine out of the reach of small children and make sure there is no trailing cable.
10 Unplug the machine before cleaning or moving it, and when it is not in use. Allow the bread machine to cool completely before cleaning and storing it.

THREE CHOCOLATE BREAD

If you like chocolate, you'll adore this bread. The recipe suggests three specific types of chocolate, but you can combine your own favourites.

SMALL

150ml/generous 5fl oz/scant ⅔ cup water
1 egg
375g/13oz/3¼ cups unbleached white bread flour
15ml/1 tbsp caster (superfine) sugar
2.5ml/½ tsp salt
20g/¾oz/1½ tbsp butter
5ml/1 tsp easy-blend (rapid-rise) dried yeast
40g/1½oz plain (semisweet) chocolate with raisins and almonds
40g/1½oz plain (semisweet) chocolate with ginger
50g/2oz Belgian milk chocolate

MEDIUM

240ml/8½fl oz/generous 1 cup water
1 egg
500g/1lb 2oz/4½ cups unbleached white bread flour
25g/1oz/2 tbsp caster sugar
5ml/1 tsp salt
25g/1oz/2 tbsp butter
7.5ml/1½ tsp easy-blend dried yeast
50g/2oz plain chocolate with raisins and almonds
50g/2oz plain chocolate with ginger
75g/3oz Belgian milk chocolate

LARGE

290ml/10¼fl oz/1¼ cups water
2 eggs
675g/1½lb/6 cups unbleached white bread flour
40g/1½oz/3 tbsp caster sugar
7.5ml/1½ tsp salt
40g/1½oz/3 tbsp butter
7.5ml/1½ tsp easy-blend dried yeast
75g/3oz plain chocolate with raisins and almonds
75g/3oz plain chocolate with ginger
115g/4oz Belgian milk chocolate

MAKES 1 LOAF

COOK'S TIP
Gradually add the chocolate to the bread machine pan, making sure that it is mixing into the dough before adding more.

1 Pour the water into the bread pan and add the egg(s). If necessary for your machine, reverse the order in which you add the liquid and dry ingredients.

2 Sprinkle over the flour, ensuring that it covers the water. Add the sugar, salt and butter, placing them in separate corners of the bread pan. Make a small indent in the centre of the flour; add the easy-blend dried yeast.

3 Set the bread machine to the basic/normal setting, with raisin setting (if available), medium crust. Press Start. Coarsely chop all the chocolate (it is not necessary to keep them separate). Add when the machine beeps, or after the first kneading (see Cook's Tip).

4 Remove the bread at the end of the baking cycle and turn out on to a wire rack to cool.

Sweet Breads & Yeast Cakes

ADAPTING RECIPES FOR USE IN A BREAD MACHINE

After you have cooked a number of the recipes from this book you may wish to branch out and adapt some of your own favourites. This sample recipe is used to explain some of the factors you will need to take into consideration.

INGREDIENTS

Read the list of ingredients carefully before you start, and adjust if necessary.

MALT EXTRACT AND GOLDEN SYRUP

High sugar levels and/or dried fruit may cause the bread to over-brown. Reduce the malt extract and golden syrup quantities by one-third and increase other liquids to compensate. Machine breads require the inclusion of sugar. Allow 5–10ml/1–2 tsp per 225g/8oz/2 cups flour.

BUTTER

High fat levels mean that the bread will take longer to rise. Reduce to 50g/2oz/¼ cup per 450g/1lb/4 cups flour. You may need to add an extra 30ml/2 tbsp liquid.

FLOUR

This recipe uses white flour, but remember a wholemeal (whole-wheat) loaf works better if you replace half the wholemeal flour with strong white bread flour.

YEAST

Replace fresh yeast with easy-blend (rapid-rise) dried yeast. In a wholemeal bread, start by using 5ml/1 tsp for up to 375g/13oz/3¼ cups flour or 7.5ml/1½ tsp for up to 675g/1½lb/6 cups flour.

MILK

Use skimmed milk at room temperature where possible. If you wish to use the time delay cycle you should replace fresh milk with milk powder.

DRIED FRUIT

Additions that enrich the dough, such as dried fruits, nuts, seeds and wholegrains, make the dough heavier, and the bread will not rise as well. Limit them to about a quarter of the total flour quantity.

MALTED FRUIT LOAF

50g/2oz/scant ¼ cup malt extract
30ml/2 tbsp golden (light corn) syrup
75g/3oz/6 tbsp butter
450g/1lb/4 cups unbleached white bread flour
5ml/1 tsp mixed (apple pie) spice
20g/¾oz fresh yeast
150ml/5fl oz/⅝ cup lukewarm milk, plus 30ml/2 tbsp milk for glazing
50g/2oz/¼ cup currants
50g/2oz/⅓ cup sultanas (golden raisins)
50g/2oz/¼ cup ready-to-eat dried apricots
25g/1oz/2 tbsp mixed chopped (candied) peel
30ml/2 tbsp caster (superfine) sugar

MAKES 2 LOAVES

1 Grease two 450g/1lb loaf tins (pans).
2 Melt the malt extract, syrup and butter in a saucepan. Leave to cool.
3 Sift the flour and spice into a large bowl; make a central well. Cream the yeast with a little of the milk; blend in the rest. Add the yeast mixture with the malt extract to the flour and make a dough.
4 Knead on a floured surface until smooth and elastic, about 10 minutes. Place in an oiled bowl; cover with oiled clear film (plastic wrap). Leave to rise in a warm place for 1½–2 hours, until doubled in bulk.
5 Turn the dough out on to a lightly floured surface and knock back.
6 Gently knead in the dried fruits.
7 Divide the dough in half; shape into two loaves. Place in the tins and cover with oiled clear film. Leave to rise for 1–1½ hours or until the dough reaches the top of the tins.
8 Meanwhile, preheat the oven to 200°C/400°F/Gas 6. Bake the loaves for 35–40 minutes, or until golden. When cooked, transfer to a wire rack.
9 Gently heat the milk and sugar for the glaze in a saucepan. Brush the warm loaves with the glaze.

METHOD

Use a similar bread machine recipe as a guide for adapting a conventional recipe.

STEP 1

Obviously, you can only make one machine-baked loaf at a time. Make 1 large loaf or reduce the quantity of ingredients if your machine is small.

STEP 2

There is no need to melt the ingredients before you add them, but remember to chop the butter into fairly small pieces.

STEP 3

When adding ingredients to the bread pan, pour in the liquid first then sprinkle over the flour, followed by the mixed spice. (Add the liquid first unless your machine requires dry ingredients to be placed in the bread pan first.)

Add easy-blend dried yeast to a small indent in the flour, but make sure it does not touch the liquid underneath.

Place salt and butter in separate corners of the pan. If your recipe calls for egg, add this with the water or other liquid.

Use water straight from the tap and other liquids at room temperature.

STEPS 4–8

Ignore these steps, apart from step 6. The bread machine will automatically mix, rise and cook the dough. Use a light setting for the crust due to the sugar, fat and fruit content of the Malted Fruit Loaf. Ordinary breads, such as a white loaf, need a medium setting; loaves that contain wholemeal flour should be baked on the whole wheat setting.

If you are adding extra ingredients, such as dried fruit, set the bread machine on raisin setting and add the ingredients when it beeps. If you do not have this facility, add approximately 5 minutes before the end of the kneading cycle.

STEP 9

Make the glaze as usual and brush over the loaf at the end of the baking cycle.

CRANBERRY AND ORANGE BREAD

The distinctive tart flavour of cranberries is intensified when these American fruits are dried. They combine well here with orange rind and pecan nuts.

1 Pour the water, orange juice and egg(s) into the bread machine pan. If the instructions for your machine specify that the yeast is to be placed in the pan first, reverse the order in which you add the liquid and dry ingredients.

2 Sprinkle over the flour, ensuring that it covers the water. Add the skimmed milk powder. Place the sugar, salt and butter in separate corners of the bread pan. Make a small indent in the centre of the flour (but not down as far as the liquid) and add the yeast.

3 Set the bread machine to the basic/normal setting, with raisin setting (if available), medium crust. Press Start. Add the orange rind, cranberries and pecan nuts when the machine beeps, or after the first kneading.

4 Remove the bread from the pan at the end of the baking cycle and turn out on to a wire rack. Mix the orange juice and caster sugar in a small pan. Heat, stirring, until the sugar dissolves, then boil until syrupy. Brush the syrup over the loaf and leave to cool.

SMALL
70ml/2½ fl oz/scant 5 tbsp water
80ml/scant 3 fl oz/⅓ cup orange juice
1 egg
375g/13oz/3¼ cups unbleached white bread flour
15ml/1 tbsp skimmed milk powder (non fat dry milk)
40g/1½oz/3 tbsp caster (superfine) sugar
2.5ml/½ tsp salt
25g/1oz/2 tbsp butter
5ml/1 tsp easy-blend (rapid-rise) dried yeast
10ml/2 tsp grated orange rind
40g/1½oz/⅓ cup dried cranberries
25g/1oz/¼ cup pecan nuts, chopped

MEDIUM
120ml/4fl oz/½ cup water
120ml/4fl oz/½ cup orange juice
1 egg
500g/1lb 2oz/4½ cups unbleached white bread flour
30ml/2 tbsp skimmed milk powder
50g/2oz/¼ cup caster sugar
3.5ml/¾ tsp salt
40g/1½oz/3 tbsp butter
7.5ml/1½ tsp easy-blend dried yeast
15ml/1 tbsp grated orange rind
50g/2oz/scant ½ cup dried cranberries
40g/1½oz/3 tbsp pecan nuts, chopped

LARGE
140ml/5fl oz/scant ⅔ cup water
150ml/5fl oz/⅔ cup orange juice
2 eggs
675g/1½lb/6 cups unbleached white bread flour
45ml/3 tbsp skimmed milk powder
65g/2½oz/5 tbsp caster sugar
5ml/1 tsp salt
50g/2oz/¼ cup butter
7.5ml/1½ tsp easy-blend dried yeast
20ml/4 tsp grated orange rind
75g/3oz/⅔ cup dried cranberries
50g/2oz/½ cup pecan nuts, chopped

FOR GLAZING
30ml/2 tbsp each fresh orange juice and caster sugar

MAKES 1 LOAF

USEFUL GUIDELINES

Here are a few guidelines that are worth following when adapting your own favourite recipes.

• Make sure the quantities will work in your machine. If you have a small bread machine it may be necessary to reduce them. Use the flour and water quantities in recipes in the book as a guide, or refer back to your manufacturer's handbook.

• It is important that you keep the flour and the liquid in the correct proportions, even if reducing the quantities means that you end up with some odd amounts. You can be more flexible with spices and flavourings such as fruit and nuts, as exact quantities are not so crucial.

• Monitor the recipe closely the first time you make it and jot down any ideas you have for improvements next time.

• Check the consistency of the dough when the machine starts mixing. You may need to add one or two extra spoonfuls of water, as breads baked in a machine

BELOW: Use a similar bread machine recipe to help you adapt a bread you usually make conventionally. For example, if you have a favourite swede bread recipe, try adapting a machine recipe for parsnip bread.

ABOVE: Some conventional recipes call for you to knead ingredients, such as fried onions, into a dough. When adapting for a bread machine, add to the dough at the raisin beep.

require a slightly softer dough, which is wet enough to relax back into the shape of the bread pan.

• If a dough mixes perfectly in your machine but then fails to bake properly, or if you want bread of a special shape, use the dough cycle on your machine, then shape by hand before baking in a conventional oven.

• Look through bread machine recipes and locate something that is similar. This will give you some idea as to quantities, and which programme you should use. Be prepared to make more adjustments after testing your recipe for the first time.

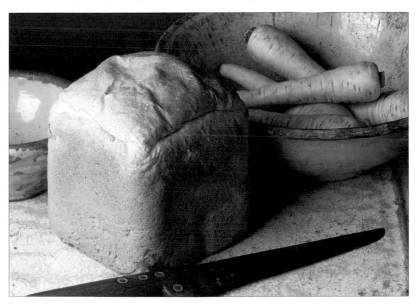

USING BREAD MIXES

Packaged bread mixes can be used in your machine. Check your handbook, as some manufacturers may recommend specific brands.

• Check that your machine can handle the amount of dough the bread mix makes. If the packet quantity is only marginally more than you usually make, use the dough cycle and then bake the bread conventionally.

• Select an appropriate setting; for instance, use the normal or rapid setting for white bread.

1 Place the recommended amount of water in the bread pan.

2 Spoon over the bread mix and place the pan in the machine.

3 Select the programme required and press Start. Check the consistency of the dough after 5 minutes, adding a little more water if the mixture seems too dry.

4 At the end of the baking cycle, remove the cooked bread from the bread pan and turn out on to a wire rack to cool.

BLUEBERRY AND OATMEAL BREAD

The blueberries add a subtle fruitiness to this loaf, while the oatmeal contributes texture and a nutty flavour. This is best eaten on the day it is baked, which shouldn't be a problem.

SMALL

75ml/5 tbsp water

75ml/5 tbsp milk

1 egg

325g/11½oz/scant 3 cups unbleached white bread flour, plus 30ml/2 tbsp for coating the blueberries

25g/1oz/¼ cup coarse oatmeal

5ml/1 tsp mixed (apple pie) spice

40g/1½oz/3 tbsp caster (superfine) sugar

2.5ml/½ tsp salt

25g/1oz/2 tbsp butter

5ml/1 tsp easy-blend (rapid-rise) dried yeast

50g/2oz/½ cup blueberries

MEDIUM

110ml/scant 4 fl oz/scant ½ cup water

120ml/4fl oz/½ cup milk

1 egg

450g/1lb/4 cups unbleached white bread flour, plus 30ml/2 tbsp for coating the blueberries

50g/2oz/½ cup coarse oatmeal

7.5ml/1½ tsp mixed spice

50g/2oz/¼ cup caster sugar

3.5ml/¾ tsp salt

40g/1½oz/3 tbsp butter

7.5ml/1½ tsp easy-blend dried yeast

75g/3oz/¾ cup blueberries

LARGE

140ml/5fl oz/scant ⅔ cup water

150ml/5fl oz/⅔ cup milk

2 eggs

625g/1lb 6oz/5½ cups unbleached white bread flour, plus 30ml/2 tbsp for coating the blueberries

50g/2oz/½ cup coarse oatmeal

10ml/2 tsp mixed spice

65g/2½oz/5 tbsp caster sugar

3.5ml/¾ tsp salt

50g/2oz/¼ cup butter

10ml/2 tsp easy-blend dried yeast

100g/3½oz/scant 1 cup blueberries

MAKES 1 LOAF

COOK'S TIP
Use the light crust setting if your bread machine produces a rich, fairly dark crust in a sweet loaf.

1 Pour the water, milk and egg(s) into the bread machine pan. If the instructions for your machine specify that the yeast is to be placed in the pan first, reverse the order in which you add the liquid and dry ingredients.

2 Sprinkle over the flour, ensuring it covers the liquid. Add the oatmeal and spice. Add the sugar, salt and butter in separate corners. Make a small indent in the centre of the flour (but not down as far as the liquid) and add the yeast.

3 Set the bread machine to the basic/normal setting, with raisin setting (if available), medium crust. Press Start. Toss the berries with the extra flour to coat. Add to the dough when the machine beeps, or after the first kneading.

4 Remove the bread from the pan at the end of the baking cycle and turn out on to a wire rack to cool.

TROUBLESHOOTING

Bread machines are incredibly easy to use and, once you have become familiar with yours, you will wonder how you ever did without it. However, they are machines and they cannot think for themselves. Things can go wrong and you need to understand why. Here are a few handy troubleshooting tips.

BREAD RISES TOO MUCH

• Usually caused by too much yeast; reduce by 25 per cent.
• An excess of sugar will promote yeast action; try reducing the quantity of sugar.
• Did you leave out the salt or use less than was recommended? If so, the yeast would have been uncontrolled and a tall loaf would have been the likely result.
• Too much liquid can sometimes cause a loaf to over-rise. Try reducing by 15–30ml/ 1–2 tbsp next time.
• Other possibilities are too much dough or too hot a day.

BREAD DOES NOT RISE ENOUGH

• Insufficient yeast or yeast that is past its expiry date.
• A rapid cycle was chosen, giving the bread less time to rise.

• The yeast and salt came into contact with each other before mixing. Make sure they are placed in separate areas when added to the bread pan.
• Too much salt inhibits the action of the yeast. You may have added salt twice, or added other salty ingredients, such as ready-salted nuts or feta cheese.
• Wholegrain and wholemeal (whole-wheat) breads tend not to rise as high as white flour breads. Their bran and wheat germ makes the flour heavier.
• You may have used a plain (all-purpose) white flour instead of a strong bread flour, which has a higher gluten content.
• The ingredients were not at the correct temperature. If they were too hot, they may have killed the yeast; if they were too cold, they may have retarded the action of the yeast.
• Insufficient liquid. In order for dough to rise adequately, it needs to be soft and pliable. If the dough was dry and stiff, add more liquid next time.
• The lid was open during the rising stage for long enough to let warm air escape.
• No sugar was added. Yeast works better where there is at least 5ml/1 tsp sugar to feed it. Note, however, that high sugar levels may retard yeast action.

BREAD DOES NOT RISE AT ALL
• No yeast was added or it was past its expiry date.
• The yeast was not handled correctly and was probably killed by adding ingredients that were too hot.

THE DOUGH IS CRUMBLY AND DOESN'T FORM A BALL
• The dough is too dry. Add extra liquid a small amount at a time until the ingredients combine to form a pliable dough.

THE DOUGH IS VERY STICKY AND DOESN'T FORM A BALL
• The dough is too wet. Try adding a little extra flour, a spoonful at a time, waiting for it to be absorbed before adding more. You must do this while the machine is still mixing and kneading the dough.

BREAD MIXED BUT NOT BAKED
• A dough cycle was selected. Remove the dough, shape it and bake it in a conventional oven or bake it in the machine on the "bake only" cycle.

BREAD COLLAPSED AFTER RISING OR DURING BAKING
• Too much liquid was added. Reduce the amount by 15–30ml/1–2 tbsp next time, or add a little extra flour.
• The bread rose too much. Reduce the amount of yeast slightly in the future, or use a quicker cycle.
• Insufficient salt. Salt helps to prevent the dough from over-proving.
• The machine may have been placed in a draught or may have been knocked or jolted during rising.
• High humidity and warm weather may have caused the dough to rise too fast.
• Too much yeast may have been added.
• The dough may have contained a high proportion of cheese.

THERE ARE DEPOSITS OF FLOUR ON THE SIDES OF THE LOAF

• The dry ingredients, especially the flour, stuck to the sides of the pan during kneading, and then adhered to the rising dough. Next time, use a flexible rubber spatula to scrape down the sides of the pan after 5–10 minutes of the initial mixing cycle, if necessary, but take care to avoid the kneading blade.

CRUST IS SHRIVELLED OR WRINKLED
• Moisture condensed on top of the loaf while it was cooling. Remove from the bread machine as soon as it is cooled.

SWEET BREADS & YEAST CAKES

Fresh fruit-flavoured loaves and rich yeast cakes filled with nuts, dried fruits or chocolate are all part of this diverse range of breads. A bread machine is the perfect tool for mixing and proving the rich doughs of Continental specialities, which are often prepared for special occasions.

CRUMBLY, COARSE TEXTURE

• The bread rose too much; try reducing the quantity of yeast slightly next time.
• The dough didn't have enough liquid.
• Too many whole grains were added. These soaked up the liquid. Next time, either soak the whole grains in water first or increase the general liquid content.

BURNT CRUST

• There was too much sugar in the dough. Use less or try a light crust setting for sweet breads.
• Choose the sweet bread setting if the machine has this option.

PALE LOAF

• Add milk, either dried or fresh, to the dough. This encourages browning.
• Set the crust colour to dark.
• Increase the sugar slightly.

CRUST TOO CHEWY AND TOUGH

• Increase the butter or oil and milk.

BREAD NOT BAKED IN THE CENTRE OR ON TOP

• Too much liquid was added; next time, reduce the liquid by 15ml/1 tbsp or add a little extra flour.
• The quantities were too large and your machine could not cope with the dough.
• The dough was too rich; it contained too much fat, sugar, eggs, nuts or grains.
• The bread machine lid was not closed properly, or the machine was used in too cold a location.
• The flour may have been too heavy. This can occur when you use rye, bran and wholemeal flours. Replace some of it with white bread flour next time.

CRUST TOO SOFT OR CRISP

• For a softer crust, increase the fat and use milk instead of water. For a crisper crust, do the opposite.
• Use the French bread setting for a crisper crust.
• Keep a crisper crust by lifting the bread out of the pan and turn it out on to a wire rack as soon as the baking cycle finishes.

AIR BUBBLE UNDER THE CRUST

• The dough was not mixed well or didn't deflate properly during the knock-down cycle between risings. This is likely to be a one-off problem, but if it persists, try adding an extra spoonful of water.

ADDED INGREDIENTS WERE CHOPPED UP INSTEAD OF REMAINING WHOLE

• They were added too soon and were chopped by the kneading blade. Add on the machine's audible signal, or 5 minutes before the end of the kneading cycle.
• Leave chopped nuts and dried fruits in larger pieces.

ADDED INGREDIENTS NOT MIXED IN

• They were probably added too late in the kneading cycle. Next time, add them a couple of minutes sooner.

THE BREAD IS DRY

• The bread was left uncovered to cool too long and dried out.
• Breads low in fat dry out rapidly. Increase the fat or oil in the recipe.
• The bread was stored in the refrigerator. Next time place in a plastic bag when cool and store in a bread bin.

BREAD HAS A HOLEY TEXTURE

• The dough was too wet; use less liquid.
• Salt was omitted.
• Warm weather and/or high humidity caused the dough to rise too quickly.

A STICKY LAYERED UNRISEN MESS

• You forgot to put the kneading blade in the pan before adding the ingredients.
• The kneading blade was not correctly inserted on the shaft.
• The bread pan was incorrectly fitted.

SMOKE EMITTED FROM THE MACHINE

• Ingredients were spilt on the heating element. Remove the bread pan before adding ingredients, and add any extra ingredients carefully.

OTHER FACTORS

Creating the ideal conditions for your bread machine is largely a matter of trial and error. Take into account the time of year, the humidity and your altitude. Bread machines vary between models and manufacturers, and flour and yeast may produce slightly different results from brand to brand or country to country. Breads made in Australia, for example, often need slightly more water than those made in Britain.

You will soon get to know your machine. Watch the dough as it is mixing and check again before it begins to bake. Make a note of any tendencies (do you generally need to add more flour? does the bread often over-rise?) and adapt recipes accordingly.

MARZIPAN AND ALMOND TWISTS

90ml/6 tbsp water
1 egg
60ml/4 tbsp Amaretto liqueur
350g/12oz/3 cups unbleached white bread flour
30ml/2 tbsp skimmed milk powder (non fat dry milk)
40g/1½oz/3 tbsp caster (superfine) sugar
2.5ml/½ tsp salt
50g/2oz/¼ cup butter, melted
7.5ml/1½ tsp easy-blend (rapid-rise) dried yeast
115g/4oz/1 cup ground almonds
50g/2oz/½ cup icing (confectioners') sugar
2–3 drops of almond essence (extract)
1 egg, separated
10ml/2 tsp milk
flaked (sliced) almonds, for sprinkling

MAKES 9

If you like almonds, you'll love these. Amaretto liqueur, marzipan and flaked almonds make up a triple whammy.

1 Pour the water, egg and Amaretto into the bread machine pan. If the instructions for your machine specify that the yeast is to be placed in the pan first, reverse the order in which you add the liquid and dry ingredients.

2 Sprinkle over the flour, ensuring that it covers the liquid. Add the skimmed milk powder. Place the sugar, salt and butter in separate corners of the bread pan. Make a small indent in the centre of the flour (but not down as far as the liquid) and pour the easy-blend dried yeast into the hollow.

3 Set the bread machine to the dough setting; use basic dough setting (if available). Press Start. Lightly grease two baking sheets and set aside.

4 Make the marzipan filling. Mix the ground almonds, icing sugar, almond essence, egg white and 15ml/3 tsp water in a bowl and set aside. In a separate bowl, beat the egg yolk with 10ml/2 tsp water.

5 When the dough cycle has finished, remove the dough from the machine and place it on a lightly floured surface. Knock it back (punch it down) gently and then roll it out into a 45 × 23cm/18 × 9in rectangle. Cut this in half lengthways to make two 23cm/9in squares.

6 Spread the filling over one of the squares to cover it completely. Brush some beaten egg yolk mixture over the remaining square and place it egg side down on top of the marzipan filling.

7 Cut nine strips, each 2.5cm/1in wide. Cut a lengthways slit near the end of one of the strips. Twist the strip, starting from the uncut end, then pass the end through the slit and seal the ends together, with egg mixture. Repeat with the remaining strips.

8 Place the twists on the baking sheets and cover with oiled clear film (plastic wrap). Leave in a warm place to rise for 30 minutes or until doubled in size.

9 Meanwhile, preheat the oven to 200°C/400°F/Gas 6. Mix the remaining egg yolk mixture with the milk and brush the mixture over the twists to glaze. Sprinkle with a few flaked almonds and bake for 12–15 minutes, or until golden. Turn out on to a wire rack to cool.

FLOUR

The largest single ingredient used in bread, the right flour is the key to good bread making. Wheat is the primary grain for grinding into flour. Apart from rye, wheat is the only flour with sufficient gluten to make a well-leavened bread.

WHEAT FLOURS

Wheat consists of an outer husk or bran that encloses the wheat kernel. The kernel contains the wheat germ and the endosperm, which is full of starch and protein. It is these proteins that form gluten when flour is mixed with water. When dough is kneaded, gluten stretches like elastic to trap the bubbles of carbon dioxide, the gas released by the action of the yeast, and the dough rises.

Wheat is defined as either soft or hard, depending on its protein content, and is milled in various ways to give the wide range of flours we know today.

Wheat is processed to create many sorts of flour. White flours, for example, contain about 75 per cent of the wheat kernel. The outer bran and the wheat germ are removed to leave the endosperm, which is milled into a white flour. Unbleached flour is the best type to use, as it has not been chemically treated to make it unnaturally white. This type is gradually replacing much of the bleached flour.

ABOVE: Clockwise from top left: Granary, stoneground strong wholemeal, strong brown, stoneground wholemeal

PLAIN WHITE FLOUR

A plain (all-purpose) white flour contains less protein and gluten than bread flour, typically around 9.5–10 per cent. Sometimes a small amount of this type of flour is mixed with bread flour to achieve a closer-grained texture, but the main use for plain white flour is in quick teabreads, when chemical raising agents such as baking powder are added to give a light, airy crumb.

STRONG WHITE BREAD FLOUR

This flour is milled from hard wheat flour, which has a higher protein level than soft wheat flour. Levels vary between millers but the typical figure is around 12 per cent. Some types of bread flour have lower levels – around 10.5–11 per cent – but these have ascorbic acid added to act as a dough enhancer.

SELF-RAISING FLOUR

This is not used in traditional breads, but self-raising (self-rising) flour is ideal for quick teabreads and cakes cooked in the bread machine. Sodium bicarbonate and calcium phosphate are mixed into the flour and act as raising agents.

FINE FRENCH PLAIN FLOUR

Used principally for baking in France, this unbleached light flour is very fine and thus free-flowing. A small amount is often added to French bread recipes to reduce the gluten content slightly and achieve a fine light texture.

RIGHT: Clockwise from top: strong, French, self-raising and plain flour

DEVONSHIRE SPLITS

A summer afternoon, a scrumptious cream tea; Devonshire splits are an essential part of this British tradition.

140ml/5fl oz/⅔ cup milk
225g/8oz/2 cups unbleached white bread flour
25g/1oz/2 tbsp caster (superfine) sugar
2.5ml/½ tsp salt
5ml/1 tsp easy-blend (rapid-rise) dried yeast
icing (confectioners') sugar, for dusting

FOR THE FILLING
clotted cream or whipped double (heavy) cream
raspberry or strawberry jam

MAKES 8

5 When the dough cycle has finished, remove the dough and place it on a lightly floured surface. Knock back (punch down) gently, then divide into eight portions.

6 Shape each portion of dough into a ball, using cupped hands. Place on the prepared baking sheets, and flatten the top of each ball slightly. Cover with oiled clear film (plastic wrap). Leave to rise for 30–45 minutes or until doubled in size.

7 Meanwhile, preheat the oven to 220°C/425°F/Gas 7. Bake the buns for 15–18 minutes, or until they are light golden in colour. Turn out on to a wire rack to cool.

8 Split the buns open and fill them with cream and jam. Dust them with icing sugar just before serving.

1 Pour the milk into the bread pan. If your machine instructions specify it, reverse the order in which you add the liquid and dry ingredients.

2 Sprinkle over the flour, ensuring that it covers the liquid completely. Add the caster sugar and salt, placing them in separate corners of the bread machine pan.

3 Make a small indent in the centre of the flour (do not go down as far as the milk underneath) and pour the easy-blend dried yeast into the hollow.

4 Set the bread machine to the dough setting; use basic dough setting (if available). Press Start. Lightly grease two baking sheets.

ORGANIC FLOURS

Organic white flour is produced using only natural fertilizers, and the wheat has not been sprayed with pesticides. Organic bread flours can be used in any recipe, and are recommended when developing natural yeasts for starters and sourdoughs.

WHOLEMEAL FLOURS

Because it is made from the complete wheat kernel, including the bran and wheat germ, wholemeal (wholewheat) is coarse textured and full-flavoured with a nutty taste. For making machine breads, use strong wholemeal bread flour, with a protein content of around 12.5 per cent. Plain wholemeal flour can be used with baking powder or bicarbonate of soda (baking soda) for teabreads. Loaves made with 100 per cent wholemeal tend to be very dense. The bran inhibits the release of gluten, so wholemeal doughs rise more slowly. Many machine recipes recommend blending wholemeal flour with white bread flour.

Stoneground flour results when complete wheat grain is ground between two stones. Wholemeal flours that are not stoneground have the bran and wheat germ removed during milling. They are replaced at the end of processing.

BROWN BREAD FLOUR

This flour contains about 80–90 per cent of the wheat kernel, with some of the bran removed. It is a good alternative to wholemeal flour, as it produces a loaf with a lighter finish, but with a denser texture and fuller flavour than white bread.

GRANARY FLOUR

A combination of wholemeal, white and rye flours mixed with malted wheat grains, this adds texture and contributes a flavour that is slightly sweet and nutty. Malthouse is similar to Granary flour.

ABOVE: Left to right: semolina, spelt

SPELT FLOUR

Rich in nutrients, this is made from spelt grain, an ancient precursor of modern wheat. It is best used in combination with white bread flour. Even though it contains gluten, some gluten-intolerant people can digest it, so it is included in some diets for people who are allergic to wheat.

SEMOLINA

A high gluten flour, semolina is made from the endosperm of durum or hard winter wheat before it is fully milled into a fine flour. It can be ground to a coarse granular texture or a finer flour. The finer flour is traditionally used for making pasta, but also makes a delicious bread when combined with other flours. If 100 per cent semolina is used, a heavy loaf will result.

OTHER WHEAT GRAINS

WHEAT BRAN

This is the outer husk of the wheat, which is separated from white flour during processing. It adds fibre, texture and flavour. You can add a spoonful or two to your favourite recipe or use it in place of part of the white bread flour.

WHEAT GERM

The germ is the embryo or heart of the wheat grain kernel. Use in its natural state, or lightly toasted, giving a nutty flavour. Wheat germ is a rich source of vitamin E and increases the nutritional value of bread. However, it inhibits the action of gluten, so do not use more than 30ml/2 tbsp for every 225g/8oz/2 cups flour.

CRACKED WHEAT

This is whole wheat kernel, broken into rather large pieces. It is quite hard, so you may like to soften it. Simmer in hot water for 15 minutes, then drain and cool. Add 15–30ml/1–2 tbsp to a dough 5 minutes before the end of the kneading cycle.

BELOW: Clockwise from top left: bran, bulgur wheat, wheat germ, cracked wheat

YORKSHIRE TEACAKES

280ml/10fl oz/scant 1¼ cups milk
450g/1lb/4 cups unbleached white
bread flour
5ml/1 tsp salt
40g/1½oz/3 tbsp caster
(superfine) sugar
40g/1½oz/3 tbsp lard (shortening)
or butter
5ml/1 tsp easy-blend (rapid-rise)
dried yeast
50g/2oz/¼ cup currants
50g/2oz/⅓ cup sultanas
(golden raisins)
milk, for glazing

MAKES 8–10

These fruit-filled tea-time treats are thought to be a refinement of the original medieval manchet or "handbread" – a hand-shaped loaf made without a tin. Serve them split and buttered, either warm from the oven or toasted.

1 Pour the milk into the bread machine pan. If the instructions for your machine specify that the yeast is to be placed in the pan first, then simply reverse the order in which you add the liquid and dry ingredients to the pan.

2 Sprinkle over the flour, ensuring that it covers the milk completely. Add the salt, sugar and lard or butter, placing them in separate corners of the bread machine pan. Make a small indent in the centre of the flour (but do not go down as far as the liquid underneath) and pour the easy-blend dried yeast into the hollow.

3 Set the bread machine to the dough setting; use basic raisin dough setting (if available). Press Start. Add the currants and sultanas when the machine beeps. If your machine does not have this facility, simply add the dried fruits 5 minutes before the end of the kneading period.

4 Lightly grease two baking sheets. When the dough cycle has finished, remove the dough from the machine and place it on a lightly floured surface. Knock it back (punch it down) gently.

5 Divide the dough into eight or ten portions, depending on how large you like your Yorkshire teacakes, and shape into balls. Flatten out each ball into a disc about 1cm/½in thick.

6 Place the discs on the prepared baking sheets, about 2.5cm/1in apart. Cover them with oiled clear film (plastic wrap) and leave in a warm place for 30–45 minutes, or until they are almost doubled in size. Meanwhile, preheat the oven to 200°C/400°F/Gas 6.

7 Brush the top of each teacake with milk, then bake for 15–18 minutes, or until golden. Turn out on to a wire rack to cool slightly.

8 To serve, split open while still warm and spread with lashings of butter, or let the buns cool, then split and toast them before adding butter.

BULGUR WHEAT

This is made from the wheat grain. It is partially processed by boiling, which cracks the wheat kernel. Add to bread doughs, to give a crunchy texture. There is no need to cook it first. However you may wish to soak it in water first, to soften it further.

NON-WHEAT FLOURS

RYE FLOUR

Rye flour is used extensively in breads, partly because it grows well in climates that are cold and wet and not suitable for wheat cultivation. This is why so many of the Russian and Scandinavian breads include rye. Light and medium rye flours are produced from the endosperm while dark rye includes all the grain, resulting in a coarser flour which adds more texture to the bread. Rye contains gluten, but when used on its own produces a very heavy bread. Rye dough is very sticky and difficult to handle. For machine-made breads, rye flour must be combined with other flours. Even a small amount adds a distinctive tang.

MILLET FLOUR

Another high-protein, low-gluten grain, millet produces a light yellow flour with a distinctly sweet flavour and a slightly gritty texture. It tends to give breads a dry, crumbly texture, so you may need to add extra fat when using it. If using millet flour, boost the gluten content of the dough by using at least 75 per cent white bread flour.

BARLEY

Barley seeds are processed to remove the bran, leaving a product called pearl barley. This is ground to make barley flour, which is mild, slightly sweet and earthy. It gives breads a soft, almost cake-like texture, as it has a very low gluten content. White flour must be combined with barley flour in a ratio of at least 3:1 for machine bread.

BUCKWHEAT FLOUR

This greyish-brown flour has a distinctive, bitter, earthy flavour. Buckwheat is the seed of a plant related to the rhubarb family. It is rich in calcium and vitamins A and B, high in protein but low in gluten. Traditionally used to make pancakes, Russian blinis and French galettes, it is best used in combination with other flours, to produce full-bodied and tasty multigrain breads.

BELOW: Top to bottom: millet, buckwheat, barley

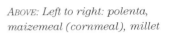

ABOVE: Left to right: polenta, maizemeal (cornmeal), millet

OTHER GRAINS

OATMEAL

When oats are cleaned and the outer husk has been removed, what remains is the oat kernel or groat. This is then cut into pieces to make either fine, medium or coarse oatmeal, or fully ground to make flour. All of these ingredients can be used in multigrain breads, adding a rich flavour and texture. The coarser the oats, the more texture they will contribute to the

ABOVE: Top to bottom: oatmeal, rye

Flour

210ml/7½fl oz/scant 1 cup milk
1 egg
450g/1lb/4 cups unbleached white
bread flour
7.5ml/1½ tsp mixed (apple pie) spice
2.5ml/½ tsp ground cinnamon
2.5ml/½ tsp salt
50g/2oz/¼ cup caster (superfine) sugar
50g/2oz/¼ cup butter
7.5ml/1½ tsp easy-blend (rapid-rise)
dried yeast
75g/3oz/scant ½ cup currants
25g/1oz/3 tbsp sultanas (golden raisins)
25g/1oz/3 tbsp cut mixed (candied) peel

For the Pastry Crosses
50g/2oz/½ cup plain (all-purpose) flour
25g/1oz/2 tbsp margarine

For the Glaze
30ml/2 tbsp milk
25g/1oz/2 tbsp caster sugar

Makes 12

1 Pour the milk and egg into the bread pan. Reverse the order in which you add the liquid and dry ingredients if your machine requires this.

2 Sprinkle over the flour, ensuring that it covers the liquid. Add the mixed spice and cinnamon. Place the salt, sugar and butter in separate corners of the pan. Make a shallow indent in the centre of the flour and add the yeast.

COOK'S TIP
If preferred, to make the crosses roll out 50g/2oz shortcrust (unsweetened) pastry, and cut into narrow strips. Brush the buns with water to attach the crosses.

HOT CROSS BUNS

The traditional cross on these Easter buns originates from early civilization and probably symbolized the four seasons; it was only later used to mark Good Friday and the Crucifixion.

3 Set the bread machine to the dough setting; use basic raisin dough setting (if available). Press Start. Lightly grease two baking sheets.

4 Add the dried fruit and peel when the machine beeps or 5 minutes before the end of the kneading period.

5 When the dough cycle has finished, remove the dough from the machine and place it on a lightly floured surface. Knock it back (punch it down) gently, then divide it into 12 pieces. Cup each piece between your hands and shape it into a ball. Place on the prepared baking sheets, cover with oiled clear film (plastic wrap) and leave for 30–45 minutes or until almost doubled in size.

6 Meanwhile, preheat the oven to 200°C/400°F/Gas 6. Make the pastry for the crosses. In a bowl, rub the flour and margarine together until the mixture resembles fine breadcrumbs. Bind with enough water to make a soft pastry which can be piped.

7 Spoon the pastry into a piping bag fitted with a plain nozzle and pipe a cross on each bun. Bake the buns for 15–18 minutes, or until golden.

8 Meanwhile, heat the milk and sugar for the glaze in a small pan. Stir thoroughly until the sugar dissolves. Brush the glaze over the top of the hot buns. Turn out on to a wire rack. Serve warm or cool.

bread. Oatmeal contains no gluten, so it needs to be combined with wheat flour for bread making. The coarser textured oatmeal makes an attractive topping on breads and rolls.

POLENTA AND CORNMEAL

Dried corn kernels are ground to make coarse, medium and fine meal. The medium grain is known as polenta and the fine grain as maizemeal or cornmeal. For bread making, this gluten-free flour has to be combined with white bread flour. It adds a sweet flavour and an attractive yellow colour to the dough. For shaping the bread by hand, use polenta, which is slightly coarser and adds a pleasant finish to the bread

MILLET GRAIN

This tiny, golden yellow, round grain is used in breads in Europe and Russia to give added texture. Include 15–30ml/ 1–2 tbsp in a multigrain bread, or even in a simple basic white loaf, for added interest. Millet grains make an attractive topping for many kinds of breads Millet flakes are also used in some breads.

RICE

Rice grains can be used in a variety of ways. Cooked long grain rice can be added to doughs for bread with a moist crumb. Wild rice, although strictly an aquatic grass, will add a beautiful texture and flavour. Add it near the end of the kneading cycle to keep the grain intact and give attractive dark flecks of colour to the bread. Ground rice and rice flour are milled from rice grains. Both brown and white rice flour are used, brown flour being more nutritious. Ground rice is more granular, similar to semolina. Either can replace some white bread flour in a recipe; they will add

ABOVE: Clockwise from top left: ground rice, rice flour, wild rice, long grain rice

a sweet flavour and chewy texture to the bread. Ground rice and rice flour can also be used as toppings. They are often dusted over English muffins or crumpets.

As rice is gluten-free, use only a small percentage of it with the bread flour, otherwise your loaf of bread will be rather dense.

ROLLED OATS

The inedible husk is removed from the oat kernel and the grain is then sliced, steamed and rolled to produce rolled oats. You can get jumbo-size oat flakes as well as traditional rolled porridge oats. For bread making, use old-fashioned oats rather than "quick cook" oats. Add rolled oats to bread doughs to give a chewy texture and nutty taste, or use as a topping for an attractive finish on rolls and breads.

OAT BRAN

High in soluble fibre, this is the outer casing of the oat kernel. It works like wheat germ by reducing the elasticity of the gluten, so use a maximum of 15ml/1 tbsp per 115g/4oz/ 1 cup flour. When using oat bran, you may need to add a little extra liquid to the dough.

LEFT: Clockwise from top right: jumbo oats, rolled oats, oat bran

Saffron Braids

Delicately scented and coloured with saffron, these deep-fried braids are favourite coffee-time treats in Scandinavia.

1 Heat the milk until hot but not boiling. Pour over the saffron in a bowl. Leave for 45 minutes or until cold.

2 Pour the saffron milk into the bread machine pan, then add the eggs. If the instructions for your machine specify that the yeast is to be placed in the pan first, reverse the order in which you add the liquid and dry ingredients.

3 Sprinkle over the flour, ensuring that it covers the saffron milk completely. Add the salt, sugar and butter, placing them in separate corners of the bread machine pan. Make a small indent in the centre of the flour (but do not go down as far as the liquid) and add the easy-blend dried yeast.

4 Set the bread machine to the dough setting; use basic dough setting (if available). Press Start. Lightly oil two baking sheets.

5 When the dough cycle has finished, remove the dough for the saffron braids from the bread machine and place it on a lightly floured surface. Knock it back (punch it down) gently, then divide the dough into eight pieces. Cover with a piece of oiled clear film (plastic wrap).

200ml/7fl oz/⅞ cup milk
3.5ml/¾ tsp saffron threads
2 eggs
450g/1lb/4 cups unbleached white bread flour
2.5ml/½ tsp salt
50g/2oz/¼ cup caster (superfine) sugar
50g/2oz/¼ cup butter
5ml/1 tsp easy-blend (rapid-rise) dried yeast
sunflower oil, for deep-frying
caster (superfine) sugar, for sprinkling

MAKES 8

6 Take one piece of dough (leaving the rest covered). Divide into three. Roll out each small piece into a 20cm/8in rope.

7 Place the ropes next to each other, pinch the ends together and braid them from left to right. When you reach the other end, press the ends together and tuck them under.

8 Repeat with the remaining portions of dough. Place the braid on the baking sheets. Cover with oiled clear film and leave in a warm place for 30–45 minutes or until almost doubled in size.

9 Preheat the oil for deep-frying to 180°C/360°F or until a cube of dried bread, added to the oil, turns golden brown in 30–60 seconds.

10 Fry the saffron braids two at a time for 4–5 minutes, until they are risen and golden. Drain on kitchen paper and sprinkle with caster sugar. Serve warm.

LEAVENS & SALT

Yeast is a living organism which, when activated by contact with liquid, converts the added sugar or sucrose, and then the natural sugars in the flour, into gases. These gases cause the bread to rise. As yeast is live, you must treat it with respect. It works best within the temperature range 21–36°C/70–97°F. Too hot and it will die; too cold and it will not activate. Yeast must be used before its use-by date, as old yeast loses its potency and eventually dies.

In most bread machine recipes dried yeast is used. In this book, all the recipes have been tested using easy-blend (rapid-rise) dried yeast, which does not need to be dissolved in liquid first. It is also called fast-action yeast. If you can find dried yeast especially made for use in bread machines, this will produce good results. You may need to adjust the quantities in individual recipes as variations occur between different makes of yeast.

ABOVE: Yeast is available in two forms, fresh and dried. From top to bottom: fresh yeast, dried yeast.

ABOVE: Add liquid to dissolve and activate fresh yeast.

Fresh yeast is considered by some bakers to have a superior flavour. It can be used with caution when baking in a bread machine, but is best used in the "dough only" cycle. It is hard to give exact quantities for breads, which will be made using a range of machines operating in different temperatures. The difficulty lies in preventing the bread from rising over the top of the bread pan during baking; doughs made from easy-blend dried yeast are easier to control where uniform results are required.

NATURAL LEAVENS

Long before yeast was sold commercially, sourdough starters were used to make breads. These were natural leavens made by fermenting yeast spores that occurred naturally in flour, dairy products, plant matter and spices. Breads are still produced by the same method today. Breads made using natural leavens have different flavours and textures from the breads made with commercial yeast.

BELOW: Buckwheat and Walnut Bread is made using easy-blend dried yeast, which gives good, uniform results.

ABOVE: Place dried yeast in a shallow indent in the flour.

ABOVE: Fresh yeast is dissolved before placing in the bread pan.

HAM AND CHEESE CROISSANTS

115ml/4fl oz/½ cup milk
30ml/2 tbsp water
1 egg
280g/10oz/2½ cups unbleached white bread flour
50g/2oz/½ cup fine French plain (all-purpose) flour
5ml/1 tsp salt
15ml/1 tbsp caster (superfine) sugar
25g/1oz/2 tbsp butter, plus
175g/6oz/¾ cup butter, softened
7.5ml/1½ tsp easy-blend (rapid-rise) dried yeast
1 egg yolk, to glaze
15ml/1 tbsp milk, to glaze

FOR THE FILLING
175g/6oz Emmenthal or Gruyère cheese, cut into thin batons
70g/2½oz thinly sliced dry cured smoked ham, torn into small pieces
5ml/1 tsp paprika

MAKES 12

The crispy layers of yeast pastry melt in your mouth to reveal a cheese and ham filling. Serve the croissants freshly baked and still warm.

1 Pour the milk, water and egg into the pan. Reverse the order in which you add the wet and dry ingredients, if necessary.

2 Sprinkle over the flours. Place the salt, sugar and 25g/1oz/2 tbsp butter in separate corners. Add the yeast in an indent in the flour. Set to the dough setting; use basic dough setting (if available). Press Start. Shape the softened butter into an oblong block 2cm/¾in thick.

3 When the dough cycle has finished, place the dough on a floured surface and knock back (punch down) gently. Roll out to a rectangle slightly wider than the butter block, and just over twice as long. Place the butter on one half of the pastry, fold it over and seal the edges, using a rolling pin.

4 Roll out again into a rectangle 2cm/¾in thick, twice as long as it is wide. Fold the top third down, the bottom third up, seal, wrap in clear film (plastic wrap) and chill for 15 minutes. Repeat the rolling, folding and chilling twice more, giving the pastry a quarter turn each time. Wrap in clear film and chill for 30 minutes.

5 Lightly oil two baking sheets. Roll out the pastry into a rectangle measuring 52 × 30cm/21 × 12in. Cut into two 15cm/6in strips. Using one strip, measure 15cm/6in along one long edge and 7.5cm/3in along the opposite long edge. Using the 15cm/6in length as the base of your first triangle, cut two diagonal lines to the 7.5cm/3in mark opposite, using a sharp knife. Continue along the strip, cutting six triangles in all. You will end up with two scraps of waste pastry, at either end of the strip. Repeat with the remaining strip.

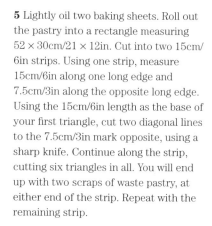

6 Place a pastry triangle on the work surface in front of you, with the pointed end facing you. Divide the cheese and ham into 12 portions and put one portion on the wide end of the triangle. Hold and gently pull each side point to stretch the pastry a little, then roll up the triangle from the filled end with one hand while pulling the remaining point gently towards you with the other hand.

7 Curve the ends of the rolled triangle away from you to make a crescent. Place this on one of the baking sheets, with the point underneath. Fill and shape the remaining croissants. Cover with oiled clear film and leave to rise for 30 minutes, until almost doubled in size. Preheat the oven to 200°C/400°F/Gas 6.

8 Mix the egg yolk and milk for the glaze and brush over the croissants. Bake for 15–20 minutes, until golden. Turn out on to a wire rack. Serve warm.

CHEMICAL LEAVENS

Raising agents other than yeasts can be used for bread. When using a bread machine, other raising agents are best used for teabreads and cakes that are mixed in a bowl, then baked in the bread pan.

Bicarbonate of soda (baking soda) is an alkaline raising agent often used for quick breads. When moistened with liquid it gives off carbon dioxide, which makes the cake or quick bread rise. The heat from the oven cooks and sets the risen batter before it can collapse.

Cream of tartar is an acid, which is often combined with bicarbonate of soda to boost the latter's leavening qualities. It also helps to neutralize the slightly soapy taste from the bicarbonate of soda.

BELOW: Bicarbonate of soda is the raising agent used for this apricot, prune and peach teabread

Baking powder is a ready-made mixture of acid and alkaline chemicals, usually bicarbonate of soda and cream of tartar, but sometimes bicarbonate of soda and sodium pyrophosphate. All these raising agents are fast acting. The bubbles are released the moment the powder comes into contact with a liquid, so such breads must be mixed and baked quickly.

SALT

Bread without salt tastes very "flat". While it is possible to make a saltless bread (there is, in fact, a famous saltless Tuscan bread which is eaten with salty cheese or preserved meats such as salami), salt is normally an indispensable ingredient. Salt has two roles: one is to improve the flavour and the other is to act as a yeast retardant, controlling the rate of fermentation, which in turn strengthens the gluten and stops the bread from rising too much and collapsing.

When adding salt to the bread pan, it is vital to keep it away from the yeast, as concentrated salt will severely impede the activity of the yeast.

Fine table salt and sea salt can both be used in bread that is to be baked in a machine. Coarse sea salt is best used as a topping. It can be sprinkled on top of unbaked breads and rolls to give a crunchy texture and agreeable flavour.

Salt substitutes are best avoided as few of these contain sodium.

DOUGH CONDITIONERS

These are added to breads to help stabilize the gluten strands and hold the gases formed by the yeast. Chemical conditioners are often added to commercially-produced bread, and you will also find bread improvers listed among the ingredients on fast-action yeast packets.

Two natural dough conditioners which help to ensure a higher rise, lighter texture, and stronger dough are lemon juice and malt extract. Gluten strength can vary between bags of flour, so you can add some lemon juice to the dough to help to strengthen it, particularly when making wholegrain breads. You can add 5ml/1 tsp lemon juice with every 225g/8oz/2 cups bread flour without affecting the flavour of the bread.

Malt extract helps to break down the starch in wheat into sugars for the yeast to feed on and so encourages active fermentation. If you use up to 5ml/1 tsp malt extract with every 225g/8oz/2 cups bread flour you will not effect a noticeable flavour change. If you like the flavour of malt extract, you can increase the amount used.

WHOLEMEAL AND RYE PISTOLETS

A wholemeal and rye version of this French and Belgian speciality. Unless your bread machine has a programme for wholewheat dough, it is worth the extra effort of the double rising, because this gives a lighter roll with a more developed flavour.

290ml/10¼fl oz/1¼ cups water
280g/10oz/2½ cups stoneground
wholemeal (whole-wheat) bread flour
50g/2oz/½ cup unbleached white
bread flour, plus extra for dusting
115g/4oz/1 cup rye flour
30ml/2 tbsp skimmed milk powder
(non fat dry milk)
10ml/2 tsp salt + 5ml/1tsp to glaze
10ml/2 tsp caster (superfine) sugar
25g/1oz/2 tbsp butter
7.5ml/1½ tsp easy-blend (rapid-rise)
dried yeast

MAKES 12

5 Leaving the rest of the dough covered, shape one piece into a ball. Roll on the floured surface into an oval. Repeat with the remaining dough.

6 Place the rolls on the prepared baking sheets. Cover them with oiled clear film and leave them in a warm place for about 30–45 minutes, or until almost doubled in size. Meanwhile preheat the oven to 220°C/425°F/Gas 7.

7 Mix the salt with 15ml/1tbsp water for the glaze and brush over the rolls. Dust the tops of the rolls with flour.

1 Pour the water into the bread pan. If the instructions for your machine specify that the yeast is to be placed in the pan first, reverse the order in which you add the liquid and dry ingredients.

2 Sprinkle over all three types of flour, ensuring that the water is completely covered. Add the skimmed milk powder. Then add the salt, sugar and butter, placing them in separate corners of the bread pan. Make a small indent in the centre of the flour (but do not go down as far as the water underneath) and add the easy-blend dried yeast.

3 Set the bread machine to the dough setting; use wholewheat dough setting (if available). If you have only one basic dough setting you may need to repeat the programme to allow sufficient time for this heavier dough to rise. Press Start. Lightly oil two baking sheets.

4 When the dough cycle has finished, remove the dough from the bread machine pan and place it on a surface that has been lightly floured. Knock the dough back (punch it down) gently, then divide it into 12 pieces. Cover with oiled clear film (plastic wrap).

8 Using the oiled handle of a wooden spoon held horizontally, split each roll almost in half, along its length. Replace the clear film and leave for 10 minutes.

9 Bake the rolls for 15–20 minutes, until the bases sound hollow when tapped. Turn out on to a wire rack to cool.

LIQUIDS

Some form of liquid is essential when making bread. It rehydrates and activates the yeast, and brings together the flour and any other dry ingredients to make the dough. Whatever the liquid, the temperature is important for successful machine breads. If your machine has a preheating cycle, cold liquids, straight from the fridge, can be used. If not, use liquids at room temperature, unless it is a very hot day. Water from the tap, providing it is merely cool, is fine. On a very cold day, measure the water and leave it to stand in the kitchen for a while so that it acclimatizes before you use it.

WATER

Water is the most frequently used liquid in bread making. Bread made with water has a crisper crust than when milk is included. Tap water is chemically treated, and if it has been heavily chlorinated and fluorinated this may well slow down the rising. Hard water can also affect the rise, because it is alkaline, which retards the yeast. If your breads are not rising very well and you have tried other remedies, then either boil some water and let it cool to room temperature or use bottled spring water.

BELOW: Cranberry juice and orange juice may be used in teabreads.

MILK

Milk helps to enrich the dough and produces a creamy-coloured, tender crumb and golden crust. Use full-cream (whole), semi-skimmed (low-fat) or skimmed milk, according to your preference. You can also replace fresh milk with skimmed milk powder. This can be useful if you intend using the timer to delay the starting time for making bread, as, unlike fresh milk, the milk powder will not deteriorate. Sprinkle it on top of the flour in the bread pan to keep it separated from the water until mixing starts.

BUTTERMILK

Used instead of regular milk, this makes bread more moist and gives it an almost cake-like texture. Buttermilk is made from skimmed milk which is pasteurized, then cooled. After this a cultured bacteria is added which ferments it under controlled conditions to produce its slightly tangy, acidic, but pleasant flavour. This flavour is noticeable in the finished loaf.

ABOVE: Clockwise from top left: milk, buttermilk, milk powder

RICOTTA AND OREGANO KNOTS

60ml/4 tbsp ricotta cheese
225ml/8fl oz/scant 1 cup water
450g/1lb/4 cups unbleached white
bread flour
45ml/3 tbsp skimmed milk powder
(non fat dry milk)
10ml/2 tsp dried oregano
5ml/1 tsp salt
10ml/2 tsp caster (superfine) sugar
25g/1oz/ 2 tbsp butter
5ml/1 tsp easy-blend (rapid-rise)
dried yeast

FOR THE TOPPING
1 egg yolk
freshly ground black pepper

MAKES 12

The ricotta cheese adds a wonderful moistness to these beautifully shaped rolls. Serve them slightly warm to appreciate fully the flavour of the oregano as your butter melts into the crumb.

1 Spoon the cheese into the bread machine pan and add the water. Reverse the order in which you add the liquid and dry ingredients if necessary.

2 Sprinkle over the flour, ensuring that it covers the cheese and water. Add the skimmed milk powder and oregano. Place the salt, sugar and butter in separate corners of the bread pan. Make a small indent in the centre of the flour (but not down as far as the liquid) and add the yeast.

3 Set the bread machine to the dough setting; use basic dough setting (if available). Press Start. Lightly oil two baking sheets.

4 When the dough cycle has finished, remove the dough from the machine and place it on a lightly floured surface.

5 Knock the dough back (punch it down) gently, then divide it into 12 pieces and cover with oiled clear film (plastic wrap).

6 Take one piece of dough, leaving the rest covered, and roll it on the floured surface into a rope about 25cm/10in long. Lift one end of the dough over the other to make a loop. Push the end through the hole in the loop to make a neat knot.

7 Repeat with the remaining dough. Place the knots on the prepared baking sheets, cover them with oiled clear film and leave to rise in a warm place for about 30 minutes, or until doubled in size. Meanwhile, preheat the oven to 220°C/425°F/Gas 7.

8 Mix the egg yolk and 15ml/1tbsp water for the topping in a small bowl. Brush the mixture over the rolls. Sprinkle some with freshly ground black pepper and leave the rest plain.

9 Bake for about 15–18 minutes, or until the rolls are golden brown. Turn out on to a wire rack to cool.

Yogurt and Other Dairy Products

Another alternative to milk, yogurt also has good tenderizing properties. Use natural (plain) yogurt or try flavoured ones, such as lemon or hazelnut in similarly flavoured breads.

Sour cream, cottage cheese and soft cheeses such as ricotta, fromage frais and mascarpone can all be used as part of the liquid content of the bread. They are valued more for their tenderizing properties than for their flavour.

Coconut Milk

Use 50:50 with water to add flavour to sweet breads and buns.

Fruit Juices

Fruit juices such as orange, mango, pineapple or cranberry can be added to the dough for fruit-flavoured breads to enhance their fruitiness.

Vegetable Juices and Cooking Liquids

The liquid left over from cooking vegetables will add flavour and extra nutritional value to breads and is particularly useful when making savoury breads. Potato water has several benefits. The extra starch acts as an additional food for the yeast, and produces a greater rise and also a softer, longer-lasting loaf.

Vegetables themselves contain liquid juices and when added to a bread machine will alter the liquid balance.

Soaking Juices

When dried vegetables such as mushrooms, especially wild ones, and sun-dried tomatoes are rehydrated in water, a

ABOVE: Ciders, beers and liqueurs all add a rich, interesting flavour to breads.

flavoursome liquid is produced. This is much too good to waste. Rehydrate the vegetables, drain off the liquid and add it as part of the liquid in a savoury bread. In sweet breads, the liquid drained from dried fruits that have been plumped up in fruit juices, spirits and liqueurs is equally useful.

Beers, Ales, Ciders and Liqueurs

All of these can be added to bread recipes. Beers and ales, in particular, have a great affinity with dark, heavy flours. The added sugars stimulate the yeast by providing more food. Dark beers and ales impart a stronger flavour.

Eggs

If a bread recipe includes eggs, these should be considered part of the liquid content. Eggs add colour, improve the structure and give the bread a rich flavour, although they are inclined to dry out more quickly than plain bread. It is worth adding extra fat to compensate for this. All the recipes in this book use medium (US large) eggs unless stated otherwise.

ABOVE: Use soaking and cooking liquids in savoury breads.

PARKER HOUSE ROLLS

These stylish rolls were first made in a hotel in Boston, after which they are named. They are delicious served warm.

1 Pour the milk and egg into the bread machine pan. If the instructions for your bread machine specify that the yeast is to be placed in the pan first, reverse the order in which you add the liquid and dry ingredients.

2 Sprinkle over the flour, ensuring that it covers the liquid. Add the sugar, salt and 25g/1oz/2 tbsp of the melted butter, placing them in separate corners of the bread pan. Make a small indent in the centre of the flour (but do not go down as far as the liquid underneath) and add the easy-blend dried yeast.

3 Set the machine to the dough setting; use basic dough setting (if available). Press Start. Lightly oil two baking sheets.

4 When the dough cycle has finished, remove the dough from the machine, place it on a lightly floured surface and knock it back (punch it down) gently.

180ml/6½fl oz/generous ¾ cup milk
1 egg
450g/1lb/4 cups unbleached white bread flour
10ml/2 tsp caster (superfine) sugar
7.5ml/1½ tsp salt
75g/3oz/6 tbsp butter, melted
5ml/1 tsp easy-blend (rapid-rise) dried yeast

MAKES 10 ROLLS

COOK'S TIP
If you do not have a small rolling pin – and can't borrow one from a child's cooking set – use a small clean bottle or the rounded handle of a knife to shape the rolls.

5 Roll out to a 1cm/½in thickness. Use a 7.5cm/3in cutter to make ten rounds, then use a small rolling pin to roll or flatten each across the centre in one direction, to create a valley about 5mm/¼in thick.

6 Brush with a little remaining melted butter to within 1cm/½in of the edge. Fold over, ensuring the top piece of dough overlaps the bottom. Press down lightly on the folded edge.

7 Place the rolls on the prepared baking sheets, just overlapping, brush them with more melted butter and cover with oiled clear film (plastic wrap). Leave in a warm place for 30 minutes, or until doubled in size.

8 Preheat the oven to 200°C/400°F/Gas 6. Bake the rolls for 15–18 minutes, or until they are golden. Brush the hot rolls with the last of the melted butter and transfer them to a wire rack to cool.

FATS & SWEETENERS

FATS

Whether solid (butter, margarine) or liquid (oil), small amounts of fats are often added to breads. They enrich doughs and add flavour, and, with eggs, they give a soft, tender texture to the crumb. Fats help to extend the freshness of the loaf, and in rich doughs, help to cancel out the drying effect that eggs can cause.

In small amounts, fat contributes to the elasticity of the gluten, but use too much and the opposite effect will result. The fat coats the gluten strands and this forms a barrier between the yeast and flour. This slows down the action of the yeast, and hence increases the rising time. For this reason it is best to limit the amount of fat in a machine-baked bread, or risk a heavy, compact loaf.

When making rich, brioche-style bread, it is best to use the bread machine only for making the dough. It may be necessary to use the cycle twice. Afterwards, shape the dough by hand and leave it to rise for as long as required, before baking the bread conventionally.

BELOW: Left to right: olive oil, sunflower oil, hazelnut oil and walnut oil can all be used to impart a slightly different flavour to bread.

SOLID FATS

Butter, margarine or lard can all be used in small quantities (of up to 15g/½oz/ 1 tbsp) without adding any noticeable flavour to the dough. Where a recipe calls for a larger quantity of fat, use butter, preferably unsalted (sweet). If you only have salted butter, and you are using quite a lot of it, you may need to reduce the amount of salt added to the dough. Cut the butter into small pieces so that it will mix in better. Avoid letting the fat come into contact with the yeast as it may inhibit the dissolving of the yeast.

Where butter is layered in yeast pastry for croissants and Danish pastries, it is important to soften it so it has the same consistency as the dough. Although it is possible to use low-fat spreads in bread-making, there is not much point in doing so, as they may contain up to 40 per cent water and do not have the same properties as butter.

LIQUID FATS

Sunflower oil is a good alternative to butter if you are concerned about the cholesterol level, while olive oil can be used where flavour is important. Use a fruity, full-flavoured extra virgin olive oil from the first pressing of the olives.

Nut oils, such as walnut and hazelnut, are quite expensive and have very distinctive flavours, but are wonderful when teamed with similarly flavoured breads.

Fats and oils are interchangeable in many recipes. If you wish to change a solid fat for a liquid fat or oil the amount of liquid in the dough needs to be adjusted to accommodate the change. This is only necessary for amounts over 15ml/1 tbsp.

LEFT: Left to right: margarine, butter, lard

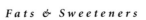

MIXED GRAIN ONION ROLLS

50g/2oz/¼ cup butter
1 large onion, finely chopped
280ml/10fl oz/1¼ cups water
280g/10oz/2½ cups unbleached white
bread flour
115g/4oz/1 cup Granary
(whole-wheat) bread flour
25g/1oz/¼ cup oat bran
10ml/2 tsp salt
10ml/2 tsp clear honey
7.5ml/1½ tsp easy-blend (rapid-rise)
dried yeast
corn meal, for dusting
30ml/2 tbsp millet grain
15ml/1 tbsp coarse oatmeal
15ml/1 tbsp sunflower seeds
MAKES 12

These crunchy rolls, flavoured with golden onions, are perfect for snacks,
sandwiches or to serve with soup.

1 Melt half the butter in a frying pan. Add the chopped onions and sauté for 8–10 minutes, or until softened and lightly browned. Set aside to cool.

2 Pour the water into the machine pan. If the instructions for your machine state the yeast is to be placed in the pan first, reverse the order in which you add the wet and dry ingredients.

3 Sprinkle over the white bread flour, Granary flour and oat bran, ensuring that the water is completely covered. Add the salt, honey and remaining butter, placing them in separate corners of the bread pan. Make a small indent in the centre of the flour (but not down as far as the liquid) and add the yeast.

4 Set the bread machine to the dough setting; use basic raisin dough setting (if available). Press Start. Lightly oil two baking sheets and sprinkle them with corn meal.

5 Add the millet grain, coarse oatmeal, sunflower seeds and cooked onion when the machine beeps. If your machine does not have this facility add these ingredients 5 minutes before the end of the kneading cycle.

6 When the dough cycle has finished, remove the dough from the bread machine and place it on a surface that has been lightly floured. Knock the dough back (punch it down) gently, then divide it into 12 equal pieces.

VARIATION
If time is short you can omit the cutting in step 9 and cook as round shaped rolls.

7 Shape each piece into a ball, making sure that the tops are smooth. Flatten them slightly with the palm of your hand or a small rolling pin. Place the rolls on the prepared baking sheets and dust them with more corn meal.

8 Cover the rolls with oiled clear film (plastic wrap) and leave them in a warm place for 30–45 minutes, or until doubled in size. Meanwhile, preheat the oven to 200°C/400°F/Gas 6.

9 Using a pair of lightly floured sharp scissors snip each roll in five places, cutting inwards from the edge, almost to the centre. Bake for 18–20 minutes, or until the rolls are golden. Turn them out on to a wire rack to cool.

*ABOVE: Left to right:
dark brown sugar;
light muscovado (brown)
sugar, soft light brown sugar;
granulated sugar, caster sugar*

SWEETENERS

Sugars and liquid sweeteners accelerate the fermentation process by providing the yeast with extra food. Modern types of yeast no longer need sugar; they are able to use the flour efficiently to provide food. Even so, it is usual to add a small amount of sweetener. This makes the dough more active than if it were left to feed slowly on the natural starches and sugars in the flour. Enriched breads and heavy whole-grain breads need the increased yeast action to help the heavier dough to rise.

Sugar helps delay the staling process in bread because it attracts moisture. It also creates a tender texture. Too much sugar can cause dough to over-rise and collapse. Sweet breads have a moderate sugar level and gain extra sweetness from dried fruits, sweet glazes and icings.

BELOW: Left to right: treacle, golden syrup, molasses, malt extract, maple syrup, honey

Sweeteners contribute to the colour of the bread. A small amount enhances the crust colour. Some bread machines over-brown sweet doughs, so select a light crust setting or a sweet bread setting, if available, when making sweet yeast cakes.

Any liquid sweetener can be used instead of sugar, but should be counted as part of the total liquid content of the bread. Adjustments may need to be made.

WHITE SUGARS

Granulated or caster (superfine) sugar can be used for bread making. They are almost pure sucrose and add little flavour to the finished bread. Do not use icing (confectioner's) sugar as the anti caking agent can affect the flavour. Save icing sugar for glazing and dusting.

BROWN SUGARS

Use light or dark brown, refined or unrefined brown sugar. The darker unrefined sugars will add more flavour, having a higher molasses content. Brown sugars add a touch of colour and also increase the acidity, which can be beneficial.

MALT EXTRACT

An extract from malted wheat or barley, this has a strong flavour, so use sparingly. It is best used in fruit breads.

HONEY AND MAPLE SYRUP

Clear honey can be used as a substitute for sugar, but only use two-thirds of the amount suggested for sugar, as it is sweeter. Maple syrup is the reduced sap of the maple tree; use it in place of honey or sugar. It is slightly sweeter than sugar but not as sweet as honey

MOLASSES, GOLDEN SYRUP AND TREACLE

All these sweeteners are by-products of sugar refining. Molasses is a thick concentrated syrup with a sweet, slightly bitter flavour. It adds a golden colour to bread. Golden (light corn) syrup is light and sweet with a slight butterscotch flavour. Treacle is brownish black and more intensely flavoured, and, like molasses, adds a slight bitterness to the bread.

PIKELETS

Pikelets are similar to crumpets, and have the same distinctive holey tops, but crumpets are thicker and are cooked inside a ring, which supports them while they set. Serve pikelets warm with preserves and butter. They are also excellent with soft cheese and smoked salmon.

140ml/5fl oz/⅝ cup water
140ml/5fl oz/⅝ cup milk
15ml/1 tbsp sunflower oil
225g/8oz/2 cups unbleached white bread flour
5ml/1 tsp salt
5ml/1 tsp caster (superfine) sugar
7.5ml/1½ tsp easy-blend (rapid-rise) dried yeast
1.5ml/¼ tsp bicarbonate of soda (baking soda)
60ml/4 tbsp water
1 egg white
MAKES ABOUT 20

5 Dissolve the bicarbonate of soda in the remaining water and stir it into the batter. Whisk the egg white in a grease-free bowl until it forms soft peaks, then fold it into the batter.

6 Cover the batter mixture with oiled clear film (plastic wrap) and leave the mixture to rise for 30 minutes. Preheat the oven to 140°C/275°F/Gas 1.

7 Lightly grease a griddle and heat it gently. When it is hot, pour generous tablespoonfuls of batter on to the hot surface, spacing them well apart to allow for spreading, and cook until the tops no longer appear wet and have acquired lots of tiny holes.

8 When the base of each pikelet is golden, turn it over, using a spatula or palette knife, and cook until pale golden.

9 Remove the cooked pikelets and layer them in a folded dishtowel. Place in the oven to keep them warm while you cook the remaining batter. Serve the pikelets immediately.

1 Pour the water into the bread machine pan, then add the milk and sunflower oil. If the instructions for your bread machine specify that the yeast is to be placed in the pan first, reverse the order in which you add the liquid and dry ingredients to the pan.

2 Sprinkle over the white bread flour, ensuring that it covers the liquid completely. Add the salt and caster sugar, placing them in separate corners of the bread pan. Make a shallow indent in the centre of the flour (but not down as far as the liquid) and add the easy-blend dried yeast.

3 Set the breadmaking machine to the dough setting; use basic dough setting (if available). Press Start. Then lightly oil two baking sheets.

4 When the dough cycle has finished, carefully lift the bread pan out of the machine and pour the batter for the pikelets into a large mixing bowl.

ADDITIONAL INGREDIENTS

MEATS

Meats can be used to flavour bread recipes. The best results often come from using cured meats, such as ham, bacon or salami, and cooked sausages such as pepperoni.

When you use a strongly flavoured meat, it is best to chop it finely and add it to the dough during its final kneading. You don't need much – 25–50g/1–2oz will be quite sufficient to add extra flavour without overpowering the bread.

Ham and bacon are best added as small pieces, late on in the kneading cycle. Dice ham small. Fry or grill (broil) bacon rashers (strips), then crumble or chop them into pieces, or sauté ready-cut cubes of bacon or pancetta. Make sure the bacon is fully cooked before adding it to bread dough.

Thinly sliced preserved meats, such as Parma ham, pastrami, speck, pepperoni and smoked venison can be added as thin strips towards the end of the kneading cycle or incorporated in the dough during shaping, for hand-shaped loaves. Cured and smoked venison marinated in olive oil and herbs gives a basic loaf of bread a wonderful burst of flavour, or you could try adding pastrami to a bread containing rye flour. Strongly flavoured meats will make the most impact, but remember that you need only small amounts.

LEFT: Sausages and bacon are a good addition to bread. They should be cooked before adding to a dough.

USING BACON IN A BREAD MACHINE

1 Cut the bacon into thin strips and grill it, or dry-fry in a non-stick frying pan, until it is crisp.

2 Transfer the cooked bacon to a plate lined with kitchen paper, to blot up excess fat. Leave to cool.

3 Add the strips to the breadmaking machine towards the end of the kneading process or when the machine beeps.

USING MEATS

Some meats are best kept whole or coarsely chopped and used as a filling, as when sausage is layered through a brioche dough, or used as a topping on tray-baked breads and pizzas. There are many different types of salami, flavoured with spices such as peppercorns, coriander or paprika, as well as pepperoni and cooked spicy Continental-style sausages, all of which are suitable.

LEFT: From top to bottom: salami, pepperoni, thinly sliced smoked venison, Parma ham

WHOLEMEAL ENGLISH MUFFINS

350ml/12fl oz/1½ cups milk
*225g/8oz/2 cups unbleached white
bread flour*
*225g/8oz/2 cups stoneground
wholemeal (whole-wheat) bread flour*
5ml/1 tsp caster (superfine) sugar
7.5ml/1½ tsp salt
15g/½oz/1 tbsp butter
*7.5ml/1½ tsp easy-blend (rapid-rise)
dried yeast*
rice flour or fine semolina, for dusting

MAKES 9

COOK'S TIP
If you don't have a griddle, cook the
muffins in a heavy frying pan. It is
important that they cook slowly.

*After a long walk on a wintry afternoon, come home to warm muffins,
carefully torn apart and spread thickly with butter.*

1 Pour the milk into the bread machine
pan. If the instructions for your bread
machine specify that the yeast is to be
placed in the pan first, then reverse the
order in which you add the liquid and
dry ingredients.

2 Sprinkle over each type of flour in
turn, making sure that the milk is
completely covered. Add the caster
sugar, salt and butter, placing each of
them in separate corners of the bread
pan. Then make a small indent in the
centre of the flour (but do not go down
as far as the liquid underneath) and add
the easy-blend dried yeast.

3 Set the machine to the dough setting;
use basic dough setting (if available).
Press Start. Sprinkle a baking sheet
with rice flour or semolina.

4 When the dough cycle has finished, place
the dough on a floured surface. Knock it
back (punch it down) gently. Roll out
the dough until it is about 1cm/½in thick.

5 Using a floured 7.5cm/3in plain cutter,
cut out nine muffins. If you like, you can
re-roll the trimmings, knead them
together and let the dough rest for a few
minutes before rolling it out again and
cutting out an extra muffin or two.

6 Place the muffins on the baking sheet.
Dust with rice flour or semolina. Cover
with oiled clear film (plastic wrap) and
leave in a warm place for 20 minutes, or
until almost doubled in size.

7 Heat a griddle over a medium heat.
You should not need any oil if the
griddle is well seasoned; if not, add the
merest trace of oil. Cook the muffins
slowly, three at a time, for about
7 minutes on each side. Serve warm.

RIGHT: From left to right: curd (farmer's) cheese, mascarpone, fromage frais

USING CHEESE IN A BREAD MACHINE

- Add a soft cheese to the bread pan with the liquids before adding the dry ingredients, unless the instructions for your breadmaking machine state that you should add dry ingredients first.
- Add grated cheese at the beginning of the dough cycle so that it becomes evenly incorporated throughout the cooked bread.

- Add coarsely crumbled cheeses when the machine beeps towards the end of the kneading, so that it retains some of its form and remains in small pockets in the dough.

CHEESES

Cheese can be added to a wide variety of breads, to make them more moist and to give them more taste. Some cheeses have powerful flavours that really impact on the bread, while others are much more subtle, and are indistinguishable from the other ingredients except for the richness and tenderness they impart. Soft cheeses such as curd (farmer's) cheese, mascarpone, fromage frais and ricotta are added in this way as part of the liquid content of the recipe. They contribute little to the overall taste of the bread, but help create a more tender loaf with a softer crumb.

Grated or chopped hard cheeses can be added at the beginning of kneading so they are totally incorporated in the dough, or else towards the end of kneading, meaning that small amounts can clearly be detected in the bread. Alternatively, the cheese can be sprinkled over the top just before baking, to add colour and texture to the crust, or used as a topping or filling, as in pizzas or calzones.

For maximum cheese flavour, use small amounts of strongly flavoured cheeses such as extra-mature Cheddar, Parmesan, Pecorino, or blue cheeses such as Roquefort, Gorgonzola, Danish Blue or Stilton.

If the cheese is salty, reduce the amount of added salt, or the action of the yeast will be retarded and the bread may taste unacceptably salty.

Machine-made breads incorporating hard cheeses may not rise as high as ones without, due to the increased richness in the dough, but the texture and flavour are likely to be superb.

RIGHT: Selection of cheeses, clockwise from top left: Cheddar, Emmenthal, feta, Gorgonzola; centre: mozzarella

ROLLS, BUNS & PASTRIES

These hand-shaped delights include French Ham and Cheese Croissants, Swedish Saffron Braids and fruity Hot Cross Buns. Devonshire Splits, Yorkshire Teacakes and Pikelets are British classics, while Parker House Rolls are a traditional American offering. Savoury rolls using mixed grains and onions, herb and ricotta-flavoured knots or Wholemeal and Rye Pistolets are just a few of the characterful small breads in this section to enjoy.

HERBS AND SPICES

Use herbs and spices as the main flavouring ingredient in bread or to enhance other ingredients.

HERBS

Fresh herbs have the most wonderful aroma, matched only by their flavour in freshly baked breads. Use fresh herbs if possible. Dried herbs that are oily and pungent, such as sage, rosemary and thyme, also work well. Rosemary is especially pungent, so use sparingly. Dried oregano is a fine substitute for fresh. Dried herbs have a more concentrated flavour than fresh; use about a third of the quantity recommended for fresh.

A number of herbs are now available freshly chopped and preserved in oil, which is a good alternative for more delicate herbs such as basil and coriander

LEFT: Clockwise from top: basil, thyme, flat leaf parsley, oregano, coriander, dill

fade with age. Use freshly grated black pepper and nutmeg. Cumin, fennel, caraway and cardamom can be bought as whole seeds, and ground in a spice mill, or a coffee mill kept for the purpose, as needed. If you buy ground spices, use them within 6 months.

Add saffron, nutmeg, cinnamon, anise, allspice and cardamom to sweet or savoury breads. Mixed spice and ginger are sweet spices, while juniper berries, cumin, coriander and black onion seeds provide aromatic flavourings for savoury breads. A number of whole spices can also be used as toppings for breads.

(cilantro), which do not dry well. Add fresh herbs toward the end of the kneading cycle. Dried herbs can be added with the dry ingredients. Avoid using dried parsley; substitute a different herb instead.

BELOW: From left to right: Front row: black onion seeds, saffron, fennel, nutmeg; back row: allspice, cinnamon, cumin, ginger

SPICES

Spices are the dried, intensely aromatic, seeds, pods, stems, bark, buds or roots of plants. As with herbs, the fresher they are the more aromatic they will be; the volatile oils

ADDING HERBS AND SPICES

- Frozen chopped herbs are a quick alternative to fresh herbs. Add them to the dough just before the end of the kneading process.
- Add ground spices after the flour, so they do not come into contact with the liquid before mixing.
- Add whole spices along with the dry ingredients if you want them to break down during kneading. If not, add them when the machine beeps, towards the end of kneading.

Additional Ingredients

Golden Pumpkin Bread

The pumpkin purée gives this loaf a rich golden crumb, a soft crust and a beautifully moist light texture, as well as a delightfully sweet-savoury flavour. It is perfect for serving with soups and casseroles.

1 Mash the pumpkin and put it in the bread machine pan. Add the buttermilk, water and oil. If the instructions for your machine specify that the easy-blend dried yeast is to be placed in the pan first, reverse the order in which you add the liquid mixture and dry ingredients.

2 Sprinkle over the flour and corn meal, ensuring that the liquid is completely covered. Add the golden syrup and salt in separate corners of the bread machine pan. Make an indent in the centre of the flour (but not down as far as the liquid) and add the yeast.

SMALL
150g/5½oz cooked pumpkin, cooled
90ml/6 tbsp buttermilk
60ml/4 tbsp water
15ml/1 tbsp extra virgin olive oil
325g/11½oz/scant 3 cups unbleached white bread flour
50g/2oz/½ cup corn meal
15ml/1 tbsp golden (light corn) syrup
5ml/1 tsp salt
4ml/¾ tsp easy-blend (rapid-rise) dried yeast
15ml/1 tbsp pumpkin seeds

MEDIUM
200g/7oz cooked pumpkin, cooled
110ml/scant 4fl oz/scant ½ cup buttermilk
45ml/3 tbsp water
30ml/2 tbsp extra virgin olive oil
425g/15oz/3¾ cups unbleached white bread flour
75g/3oz/¾ cup corn meal
22ml/1½ tbsp golden syrup
7.5ml/1½ tsp salt
5ml/1 tsp easy-blend dried yeast
22ml/1½ tbsp pumpkin seeds

LARGE
250g/9oz cooked pumpkin, cooled
150ml/5fl oz/⅔ cup buttermilk
80ml/scant 3fl oz/⅓ cup water
45ml/3 tbsp extra virgin olive oil
575g/1¼lb/5 cups unbleached white bread flour
100g/3½oz/scant 1 cup corn meal
30ml/2 tbsp golden (light corn) syrup
10ml/2 tsp salt
7.5ml/1½ tsp easy-blend dried yeast
30ml/2 tbsp pumpkin seeds

MAKES 1 LOAF

3 Set the bread machine to the basic/normal setting; use raisin setting (if available), medium crust. Press Start. Add the pumpkin seeds when the machine beeps, or during the last 5 minutes of kneading.

4 Remove at the end of the baking cycle. Turn out on to a wire rack to cool.

CHESTNUT BREAD

These quantities are for a medium loaf. Increase all ingredients by 25 per cent for a large machine; decrease by 25 per cent for a small one.

1 Put 175g/6oz/½ cup unsweetened chestnut purée in a bowl and stir in 250ml/9fl oz/scant 1¼ cups water. Mix well. Place in the bread pan.

2 Sprinkle over 450g/1lb/4 cups white bread flour and 50g/2oz/½ cup wholemeal (whole-wheat) flour. Add 30ml/2 tbsp skimmed milk powder (non-fat dry milk), 2.5ml/½tsp ground cloves and 5ml/1 tsp grated nutmeg. Place 5ml/1 tsp salt, 15ml/1 tbsp light muscovado (brown) sugar and 40g/1½oz/3 tbsp butter in separate corners. Add 7.5ml/1½tsp easy-blend (rapid-rise) dried yeast.

3 Set to the basic/normal setting, with raisin setting (if available), light crust. Press Start. Add 75g/3oz/¾ cup coarsely chopped walnuts at the beep or after the first kneading. Cool on a wire rack.

ABOVE: Clockwise from top right: pistachio nuts, pecan nuts, pine nuts, walnuts, slivered almonds, macadamia nuts

NUTS

Nuts make a wonderful addition to home-made breads. Their crunchiness combines equally well with the sweet chewiness of dried and semi-dried fruits, and with fresh fruits. They go well with savoury additions such as cheese, herbs and spices and they can be used on their own to make rustic-style breads.

Nuts contain natural oils which turn rancid if stored too warm or for too long. Buy in small quantities, store in an air-tight container in a cool place and use them within a few weeks.

Pecan nuts, almonds, macadamia nuts, pistachio nuts and walnuts give wonderful flavour and texture when added to basic breads towards the end of the kneading process. They can be added to teabreads, or used as a decoration on top of sweet breads or yeast cakes. Walnut bread is a rich brown loaf with a soft crunch, perfect with cheeses.

Lightly toast pine nuts, hazelnuts and almonds first to bring out their flavour. Spread the nuts on a baking sheet and place them in an oven preheated to 180°C/350°F/Gas 4 for 5–8 minutes, or grill until golden. Avoid scorching, and cool before adding them to the bread.

Hazelnuts, almonds and walnuts can be finely ground and used to replace up to 15 per cent of the flour with the ground nuts. If using hazelnuts, remove the skin first, as it is bitter. This will easily rub off if you toast the nuts in the oven.

Use coconut freshly grated or choose desiccated (dry unsweetened shredded), either plain or toasted.

SUN-DRIED TOMATO AND CEP LOAF

The powerful concentrated flavours of cep mushrooms and sun-dried tomatoes exude from this Mediterranean-style bread.

SMALL

10g/⅓oz dried cep mushrooms
200ml/7fl oz/⅞ cup warm water
375g/13oz/3¼ cups unbleached white bread flour
7.5ml/1½ tsp salt
15ml/1 tbsp granulated sugar
25g/1oz/2 tbsp butter
5ml/1 tsp easy-blend (rapid-rise) dried yeast
25g/1oz/¼ cup well-drained sun-dried tomatoes in olive oil

MEDIUM

15g/½oz dried cep mushrooms
200ml/7fl oz/⅞ cup warm water
500g/1lb 2oz/4½ cups unbleached white bread flour
7.5ml/1½ tsp salt
15ml/1 tbsp granulated sugar
25g/1oz/2 tbsp butter
5ml/1 tsp easy-blend dried yeast
40g/1½oz/⅓ cup well-drained sun-dried tomatoes in olive oil

LARGE

25g/1oz dried cep mushrooms
200ml/7fl oz/⅞ cup warm water
675g/1½lb/6 cups unbleached white bread flour
10ml/2 tsp salt
22ml/1½ tbsp granulated sugar
40g/1½oz/3 tbsp butter
7.5ml/1½ tsp easy-blend dried yeast
50g/2oz/½ cup well-drained sun-dried tomatoes in olive oil

MAKES 1 LOAF

1 Place the dried mushrooms in a small bowl and pour over the warm water. Leave to soak for about 30 minutes. Pour the mushrooms into a sieve placed over a bowl. Drain thoroughly, reserving the soaking liquid. Set the mushrooms aside. Make up the soaking liquid to 210ml/7½fl oz/scant 1 cup, 320ml/11fl oz/generous 1⅓ cups or 420ml/15fl oz/generous 1¾ cups, depending on the size of loaf you are making.

2 Pour the liquid into the bread pan. If necessary, reverse the order in which you add the liquid and dry ingredients.

3 Sprinkle over the flour, covering the water. Add the salt, sugar and butter, placing them in separate corners.

COOK'S TIP
Add a tablespoon or two of extra flour if the dough is too soft after adding the mushrooms and tomatoes.

4 Make a small indent in the flour; add the yeast. Set the bread machine to the basic/normal setting; use raisin setting (if available), medium crust. Press Start.

5 Chop the reserved mushrooms and the tomatoes. Add them to the dough when the machine beeps, or during the last 5 minutes of the kneading cycle.

6 Remove the bread at the end of the baking cycle and turn out on to a wire rack to cool.

VEGETABLES

Raw, canned, dried and freshly cooked vegetables all make perfect additions to savoury breads. Making bread also provides a good opportunity to use up any leftover cooked vegetables. Vegetable breads are richer than basic breads, the vegetables contributing flavour and texture to the finished loaves. Many vegetable breads are subtly coloured or dotted with attractive flecks.

Fresh vegetables are relatively high in liquid, so if you add them, calculate that about half of their weight will be water

BELOW: Clockwise from top: spinach, green, red and yellow peppers, courgettes, sweet potatoes

LEFT: Clockwise from top right: garlic, spring onions, chilli peppers, dried sliced onion, onions

and deduct the equivalent amount of liquid from the recipe. Keep an eye on the dough as it mixes and add more flour or liquid as needed.

STARCHY VEGETABLES

Potatoes, sweet potatoes, parsnips, carrots, swede and other varieties of starchy vegetables sweeten the bread and contribute a soft texture. You can use leftover mashed or even instant potato, adding 115g/4oz/1⅓ cups–225g/8oz/2⅔ cups to a basic bread recipe depending on the size of your machine. Adjust the liquid accordingly.

SPINACH

Fresh spinach leaves need to be blanched briefly in boiling water before being used. After blanching, add them whole with the liquid ingredients at the beginning

---

PREPARING PEPPERS

1 Cut each (bell) pepper into three or four flat pieces, removing the core and seeds. Place in a grill (broiler) pan or roasting tin (pan) and brush lightly with olive oil or sunflower oil.

2 Grill (broil) until the skins blister and begin to char. Remove each piece as it is cooked and place inside a plastic bag. Seal the bag and leave to cool.

3 Peel off and discard the skin, then chop the peppers and add when the bread machine beeps, or 5 minutes before the kneading cycle ends.

Additional Ingredients

BEETROOT BREAD

This spectacular bread takes on the colour of the beetroot juice. It is also flecked with beetroot flesh, which gives the finished loaf a slightly sweet flavour and delightful consistency.

150ml/5fl oz/⅔ cup water
140g/5oz/1 cup grated raw beetroot (beets)
2 spring onions (scallions), chopped
375g/13oz/3¼ cups unbleached white bread flour
15g/½oz/1 tbsp butter
7.5ml/1½ tsp salt
5ml/1 tsp granulated sugar
5ml/1 tsp easy-blend (rapid-rise) dried yeast

MEDIUM

170ml/6fl oz/¾ cup water
225g/8oz/1½ cups grated raw beetroot
3 spring onions, chopped
500g/1lb 2oz/4½ cups unbleached white bread flour
25g/1oz/2 tbsp butter
10ml/2 tsp salt
5ml/1 tsp granulated sugar
5ml/1 tsp easy-blend dried yeast

LARGE

280ml/10fl oz/1¼ cups water
280g/10oz/2 cups grated raw beetroot
4 spring onions, chopped
675g/1½lb/6 cups unbleached white bread flour
40g/1½oz/3 tbsp butter
10ml/2 tsp salt
7.5ml/1½ tsp granulated sugar
7.5ml/1½ tsp easy-blend dried yeast

MAKES 1 LOAF

3 Sprinkle the flour over the beetroot and water, ensuring it covers them both. Add the butter, salt and sugar in separate corners. Make a small indent in the centre of the flour (but not down as far as the liquid) and add the yeast.

4 Set the bread machine to the basic/normal setting, medium crust. Press Start. If you like, slash the top of the loaf with diagonal slashes just before the baking cycle starts.

5 Remove at the end of the baking cycle and turn out on to a wire rack.

1 Pour the water into the bread pan. Sprinkle over the grated beetroot. If the instructions for your machine specify that the yeast is to be placed in the pan first, reverse the order in which you add the liquid mixture and dry ingredients.

2 Add the chopped spring onions. However, if your bread machine offers you the option of adding any extra ingredients during the kneading cycle, set the spring onions aside so that you may add them later on.

Vegetable Breads

LEFT: *Fresh or dried mushrooms work well in breads*

of the kneading process, and they will mix in and become finely chopped as the cycle progresses. Frozen chopped spinach can be substituted for fresh, but thaw it completely first and reduce the liquid in the recipe to allow for the extra water.

ONIONS, LEEKS AND CHILLIES

These vegetables are best if you sauté them first in a little butter or oil, which brings out their flavour. Caramelized onions will add richness and a light golden colour to the bread. For speed, you can add dried sliced onions instead of fresh onions, but you may need to add an extra 15ml/1 tbsp or so of liquid.

MUSHROOMS

Dried wild mushrooms can be used in the same way as sun-dried tomatoes to produce a very tasty loaf for serving with soups, casseroles and stews. Strain the soaking water, if you intend to use it in a recipe, to remove any grit.

TOMATOES

Tomatoes are very versatile and give bread a delicious flavour. They can be puréed, canned, fresh or sun-dried. Depending on when you add sun-dried tomatoes they will either remain as pieces, making a bread with interesting flecks of colour, or be fully integrated in the dough to provide flavour. To intensify the taste, choose regular sun-dried tomatoes, rather than the ones preserved in oil,

reconstitute them in water, then use the soaking water as the liquid in the recipe. Other tomato products are best added at the beginning of the breadmaking cycle, to ensure a richly coloured, full-bodied loaf with a distinct tomato flavour.

OTHER VEGETABLES

Add vegetables such as corn kernels, chopped olives or chopped spring onions (scallions) towards the end of the kneading cycle to ensure they remain whole. All will impart flavour, colour and texture.

Frozen vegetables should be thawed completely before using in the machine. You may need to reduce the liquid quantity in the recipe if you use frozen vegetables instead of fresh. Canned vegetables should be well drained.

CHICKPEAS

The starchiness of chickpeas, like that of potatoes, produces a light bread with good keeping qualities. Add cooked drained chickpeas whole; the machine will reduce them to a pulp very effectively. Chickpeas add a pleasant, nutty flavour to breads.

ADDING VEGETABLES TO BREAD

There are several ways of preparing vegetables ready to add to the machine.

- Add grated raw vegetables such as carrots or beetroot(beet), when you add the water to the pan.

- Sweet potatoes, parsnips, potatoes, winter squashes and pumpkin should be cooked first. Drain, reserving the cooking liquid, and mash them. When cool, add both the cooking liquid and the mashed vegetable to the dough.

- If you want vegetables to remain identifiable in the finished bread add them when the machine beeps for adding extra ingredients or 5 minutes before the end of the kneading cycle, so they stay as slices or small pieces.

Additional Ingredients

PARSNIP AND NUTMEG BREAD

The moment you cut into this loaf, the irresistible aroma of nutmeg and parsnips fills the air. Stopping at a single slice is the tricky part.

1 Pour the water into the bread machine pan and add the mashed parsnips. If the instructions for your machine specify that the yeast is to be placed in the pan first, reverse the order in which you add the liquid mixture and dry ingredients.

2 Sprinkle over the flour, ensuring it covers the ingredients already placed in the pan. Add the milk powder and freshly grated nutmeg. Place the butter, salt and sugar in separate corners of the bread machine pan. Make a small indent in the centre of the flour (but do not go down as far as the liquid) and add the easy-blend dried yeast.

3 Set the bread machine to the basic/normal setting, medium crust. Press Start.

4 Remove the bread at the end of the baking cycle and turn out on to a wire rack to cool.

SMALL

225ml/7fl oz/scant 1 cup water
125g/4½oz/1½ cups mashed cooked parsnips
375g/13oz/3¼ cups unbleached white bread flour
15ml/1 tbsp skimmed milk powder (non fat dry milk)
2.5ml/½ tsp freshly grated nutmeg
25g/1oz/2 tbsp butter
5ml/1 tsp salt
5ml/1 tsp granulated sugar
5ml/1 tsp easy-blend (rapid-rise) dried yeast

MEDIUM

225ml/8fl oz/scant 1 cup water
175g/6oz/2 cups mashed cooked parsnips
500g/1lb 2oz/4½ cups unbleached white bread flour
30ml/2 tbsp skimmed milk powder
5ml/1 tsp freshly grated nutmeg
40g/1½oz/3 tbsp butter
7.5ml/1½ tsp salt
7.5ml/1½ tsp granulated sugar
7.5ml/1½ tsp easy-blend dried yeast

LARGE

320ml/11½fl oz/scant 1½ cups water
225g/8oz/2⅔ cups mashed cooked parsnips
675g/1½lb/6 cups unbleached white bread flour
45ml/3 tbsp skimmed milk powder
5ml/1 tsp freshly grated nutmeg
50g/2oz/¼ cup butter
10ml/2 tsp salt
10ml/2 tsp granulated sugar
7.5ml/1½ tsp easy-blend dried yeast

MAKES 1 LOAF

COOK'S TIP

Drain the parsnips thoroughly before mashing so that the dough does not become too wet. Leave the mashed parsnips to cool completely before adding them to the bread.

FRUIT

Whether you use them fresh, dried or as purées or juices, fruits add complementary flavours to breads and teacakes. The natural sugars help to feed the yeast and improve the leavening process, while fruits with natural pectin will improve the keeping quality of baked goods.

DRIED CAKE FRUITS

The familiar dried cake fruits such as sultanas (golden raisins), currants and raisins can easily be incorporated in basic breads, adding their own distinctive flavours. Sprinkle them in gradually, when the machine beeps or towards the end of the kneading cycle. For added flavour, plump them up in fruit juice or liqueur. You can add up to 50g/2oz/⅓ cup of dried fruit for a small bread machine, 115g/4oz/⅔ cup

ABOVE: Pears, bananas, apples

for a large machine. If you soak the dried fruit first, use the excess as part of the measured liquid. You may need to add a spoonful or so of extra liquid to a basic bread recipe if you do not soak the fruit first.

BELOW: Clockwise from top left: candied citrus peel, dried pears, dried cranberries, dried prunes, dried mango, and dried figs

RIGHT: Strawberries, raspberries and blueberries

DRIED, SEMI-DRIED AND READY-TO-EAT DRIED FRUITS

These are perfect for breads, because their flavours are so concentrated, and there is a vast range to choose from. Use combinations of exotic dried fruits, such as mango, papaya, melon and figs. Small dried fruits such as cranberries and cherries can be added whole, while the larger exotic fruits need to be chopped coarsely, as do apricots, pears, dates and peaches. Dried fruits such as pitted prunes can be soaked in sherry or a liqueur, as for cake fruits.

FRESH FRUITS

Some fruits such as berries can be frozen before they are added to the dough. This helps to keep them intact. Spread the fruits out in a single layer on a baking sheet and freeze them until they are solid. Add to the dough in the machine just before the end of the kneading cycle. You can also use ready-frozen fruits in this way. When adding juicy fruits, toss them with a little extra flour, to keep the consistency of the bread dough correct. Soft fruits can be added to teabread mixtures too; just fold them in at the end of mixing.

Firm fruits, such as apples or pears, can be added raw, chopped into small chunks. Plums and rhubarb can also be used raw; simply cut them into small pieces. Rhubarb can also be poached first, so that it softens slightly. You can also grate firm fruits, or mash soft ripe fruits such as bananas and pears.

COURGETTE COUNTRY GRAIN BREAD

The grated courgette combines with the flour during the kneading process to make a succulent bread, while the seeds add both texture and flavour.

1 Pour the buttermilk and water into the bread machine pan. Sprinkle over the grated courgette. If the instructions for your machine specify that the yeast is to be placed in the pan first, reverse the order in which you add the liquid and dry ingredients.

2 Sprinkle over both types of flour, ensuring the liquids are completely covered. Add the sunflower seeds, pumpkin seeds and millet seeds. Place the salt, sugar and butter in separate corners of the bread pan. Make a small indent in the flour (but not down as far as the liquid) and add the yeast.

3 Set the bread machine to the basic/normal setting, medium crust. Press Start. Just before the baking cycle, brush the top with water and sprinkle with corn meal.

4 Remove the bread at the end of the baking cycle and turn out on to a wire rack to cool.

SMALL
55ml/2fl oz/¼ cup buttermilk
70ml/2½fl oz/5 tbsp water
115g/4oz/⅔ cup grated
courgette (zucchini)
280g/10oz/2½ cups unbleached white
bread flour
50g/2oz/½ cup wholemeal
(whole-wheat) bread flour
15ml/1 tbsp sunflower seeds
15ml/1 tbsp pumpkin seeds
5ml/1 tsp millet seeds
5ml/1 tsp salt
5ml/1 tsp granulated sugar
25g/1oz/2 tbsp butter
5ml/1 tsp easy-blend (rapid-rise)
dried yeast
corn meal, for sprinkling

MEDIUM
75ml/5 tbsp buttermilk
55ml/2fl oz/¼ cup water
175g/6oz/1 cup grated courgette
375g/13oz/3¼ cups unbleached white
bread flour
75g/3oz/¾ cup wholemeal bread flour
22ml/1½ tbsp sunflower seeds
22ml/1½ tbsp pumpkin seeds
10ml/2 tsp millet seeds
7.5ml/1½ tsp salt
7.5ml/1½ tsp granulated sugar
40g/1½oz/3 tbsp butter
7.5ml/1½ tsp easy-blend dried yeast
corn meal, for sprinkling

LARGE
100ml/3½fl oz/7 tbsp buttermilk
130ml/4½fl oz/generous ½ cup water
225g/8oz/1⅓ cups grated courgette
500g/1lb 2oz/4½ cups unbleached
white bread flour
115g/4oz/1 cup wholemeal bread flour
30ml/2 tbsp sunflower seeds
30ml/2 tbsp pumpkin seeds
15ml/1 tbsp millet seeds
10ml/2 tsp salt
10ml/2 tsp granulated sugar
50g/2oz/¼ cup butter
7.5ml/1½ tsp easy-blend dried yeast
corn meal, for sprinkling

MAKES 1 LOAF

PINEAPPLE AND BANANA BREAD

These ingredient quantities are for a medium bread machine. Increase or decrease by 25 per cent as necessary.

1 Pour 60ml/4 tbsp pineapple juice and 200ml/7fl oz/⅞ cup buttermilk into the bread pan. Mash 1 large banana (about 180g/6½oz) and add. Add the dry ingredients first if your machine specifies this.

2 Sprinkle over 450g/1lb/4 cups white bread flour and 50g/2oz/½ cup wholemeal (whole-wheat) flour. Place 5ml/1 tsp salt, 45ml/3 tbsp caster (superfine) sugar and 40g/1½oz/3 tbsp butter in separate corners. Make an indent in the flour; add 5ml/1 tsp easy-blend (rapid-rise) dried yeast.

3 Set to the basic/normal setting, with raisin setting (if available), light crust. Press Start. Add 75g/3oz/½ cup chopped pineapple chunks at the beep or towards the end of the cycle. Remove from the pan and turn out on to a wire rack.

ADDING FRUIT TO BREADS

When you add the fruit and how heavily processed it is will determine whether it remains clearly detectable as whole pieces or blends fully into the dough to impart an even flavour and moistness throughout the bread.

• Add frozen orange concentrate or fruit juice right at the beginning of the mixing process, unless the instructions for your machine state you should add the dry ingredients first.

• Add purées, such as apple, pear or mango, after the water in the recipe has been poured into the bread pan. Alternatively, blend the two together first, then add the mixture to the pan.

BELOW: Fruit juice can replace part of the water quantity in some breads. Left to right: pineapple juice, apple juice, mango juice

• If you wish to add mashed or grated fruits, such as bananas or pears, put them in after the liquids.

• Add fresh or frozen whole fruits, such as berries, when the machine beeps or about 5 minutes before the end of the kneading cycle. Chopped fruits, such as apples and plums, as well as dried fruits, should also be added towards the end of the kneading process.

CHILLI BREAD

There's a warm surprise waiting for anyone who bites into this tasty wholemeal bread. Fresh chillies are speckled throughout the crumb. Use Kenyan chillies for a milder flavour or Scotch Bonnets for a fiery taste.

SMALL

15ml/1 tbsp sunflower oil
1–2 fresh chillies, chopped
210ml/7½fl oz/scant 1 cup water
250g/9oz/2¼ cups unbleached white
bread flour
125g/4½oz/generous 1 cup wholemeal
(whole-wheat) bread flour
7.5ml/1½ tsp salt
7.5ml/1½ tsp granulated sugar
25g/1oz/2 tbsp butter
5ml/1 tsp easy-blend (rapid-rise)
dried yeast

MEDIUM

15ml/1 tbsp sunflower oil
2–3 fresh chillies, chopped
320ml/11fl oz/generous 1⅓ cups water
350g/12oz/3 cups unbleached white
bread flour
150g/5½oz/1⅓ cups wholemeal
bread flour
10ml/2 tsp salt
10ml/2 tsp granulated sugar
25g/1oz/2 tbsp butter
5ml/1 tsp easy-blend dried yeast

LARGE

30ml/2 tbsp sunflower oil
3–4 fresh chillies, chopped
420ml/15fl oz/generous 1¾ cups water
475g/1lb 1oz/4¼ cups unbleached
white bread flour
200g/7oz/1¾ cups wholemeal
bread flour
10ml/2 tsp salt
15ml/1 tbsp granulated sugar
40g/1½oz/3 tbsp butter
7.5ml/1½ tsp easy-blend dried yeast

MAKES 1 LOAF

VARIATION
Use chilli flakes instead of fresh chillies, if you prefer. You will need 10–20 ml/2–4 tsp, depending on the size of the loaf and how hot you wish to make the bread.

1 Heat the oil in a small frying pan. Add the chillies and sauté them over a moderate heat for 3–4 minutes until softened. Set aside to cool.

2 Tip the chillies and their oil into the bread machine pan. Pour in the water. Reverse the order in which you add the wet and dry ingredients if necessary.

3 Sprinkle over both types of flour, ensuring that the liquid is covered. Place the salt, sugar and butter in separate corners of the bread machine pan. Make an indent in the flour (but not down as far as the liquid) and add the yeast.

4 Set the bread machine to the basic/normal setting, medium crust. Press Start.

5 Remove the bread at the end of the baking cycle and turn out on to a wire rack to cool.

EQUIPMENT

The accessories required for bread-making are quite simple, the most expensive being the bread machine, which you probably already own. The essential pieces of equipment are largely concerned with accurate measuring; the remaining items are useful for hand-shaped breads.

MEASURING

Items to measure ingredients accurately are vital for making machine-breads.

SCALES

Electronic scales give the most accurate results and are well worth investing in. You can place the bread pan directly on the scales and weigh the ingredients straight into it. The display can be set to zero after each ingredient has been added, which makes additions to the pan easy to perform and absolutely precise.

MEASURING SPOONS

Smaller quantities of dry ingredients, such as sugar, salt and, most importantly, yeast, need to be measured carefully. A set of measuring spoons from 1.5ml/¼ tsp to 15ml/1 tbsp is ideal. Always level off the ingredient in the spoon for an accurate measure.

MEASURING JUGS

Heatproof glass jugs (cups) that are clearly marked in metric and imperial units are very useful. Place the measuring jug on a flat surface to ensure accuracy, and check the level of the ingredients by bending down so the measurements are at eye level.

LEFT: Having a range of different-size glass bowls is useful.

LEFT: Bannetons may be used for final proving before the bread is baked.

LEFT: Use scales and measuring jugs, cups and spoons to ensure the correct quantity of ingredients. Accuracy is essential to give good results.

MIXING AND RISING

The bread machine will automatically mix dough and make it rise, but there may be some items of equipment you need for hand-shaped breads.

GLASS BOWLS

While most of the mixing will take place inside the machine, you will still need to mix glazes, add extra ingredients, transfer doughs or batters to a large bowl, or use a large bowl as a cover for hand-shaped bread during the final proving period. Glass bowls give all-round visibility and a selection of sizes will prove universally useful around the kitchen.

CARROT AND FENNEL BREAD

The distinctive flavour of fennel is the perfect foil for the more subtle carrot taste in this unusual bread. It looks pretty when sliced, thanks to the attractive orange flecks of carrot.

MAKES 1 LOAF

1 Pour the water, oil and honey into the bread machine pan. Sprinkle over the grated carrot. If the instructions for your machine specify that the yeast is to be placed in the pan first, reverse the order in which you add the liquid and dry ingredients.

2 Sprinkle over the flour, ensuring that it covers the water. Add the milk powder and fennel seeds. Add the salt in one corner of the bread pan. Make a small indent in the centre of the flour (but not down as far as the liquid) and add the yeast.

3 Set the machine to the basic/normal setting, medium crust. Press Start.

4 Remove at the end of the baking cycle and turn out on to a wire rack to cool.

COOK'S TIP
When adding the grated carrot, sprinkle it over lightly and evenly. This avoids clumps, which would not mix evenly through the dough.

BELOW: A French baguette tray will give French loaves their traditional shape.

LEFT: Speciality cake tins such as a kugelhopf tin and small brioche moulds may be worth acquiring.
BELOW: Assorted cake tins, fluted loose-based tart tin

dough partway through the cycle, set a kitchen timer. It is also a good idea to set a timer if the beep of your bread machine is not particularly loud and you are unlikely to be in the kitchen when the signal goes off.

BANNETON
During the final proving, breads are sometimes supported in cloth-lined baskets, called bannetons. Place baguettes in long bannetons and round loaves in round baskets. Flour the cloth well to prevent the dough from sticking. When the dough has risen you can upturn the basket and place the bread directly on a prepared baking sheet.

DISHTOWELS AND CLEAR FILM
Use a clean dishtowel or clear film (plastic wrap) to cover the dough during proving. This prevents the dough forming a dry crust. Before using, lightly flour the dishtowel or oil the clear film to prevent the dough from sticking to the cover.

TIMER
If your bread machine does not have an audible signal to remind you to add extra ingredients, or you want to remember to check the

BAKING HAND-SHAPED LOAVES
A variety of tins (pans), trays and other equipment will help you bake breads of interesting shapes or with a crispier crust.

BREAD PANS AND MOULDS
Heavy gauge baking tins and moulds are best, because they are less likely to distort in the oven. A number of shapes and sizes are useful. A 1kg or a 2lb loaf tin measuring 18.5–11.5cm/7¼ × 4½in is a good basic size and shape, or try a longer, slightly narrower tin about 23–28cm/9–10in long.

Both round and square cake tins are used for bread making, to support the dough while it rises. A 15cm/6in deep cake tin is used for baking pannetone.

RIGHT: Baking trays and loaf tins

CHICKPEA AND PEPPERCORN BREAD

Bread may be a basic food, but it certainly isn't boring, as this exciting combination proves. Chickpeas help to keep the dough light, while pink and green peppercorns add colour and "explosions" of flavour.

SMALL

200ml/7fl oz/⅞ cup water

15ml/1 tbsp extra virgin olive oil

125g/4½oz/generous ⅔ cup canned chickpeas

375g/13oz/3¼ cups unbleached white bread flour

7.5ml/1½ tsp drained fresh pink peppercorns in brine

7.5ml/1½ tsp drained fresh green peppercorns in brine

15ml/1 tbsp skimmed milk powder (non fat dry milk)

5ml/1 tsp salt

7.5ml/1½ tsp granulated sugar

5ml/1 tsp easy-blend (rapid-rise) dried yeast

milk, for brushing (optional)

MEDIUM

250ml/9fl oz/generous 1 cup water

30ml/2 tbsp extra virgin olive oil

175g/6oz/1 cup canned chickpeas

500g/1lb 2oz/4½ cups unbleached white bread flour

10ml/2 tsp drained fresh pink peppercorns in brine

10ml/2 tsp drained fresh green peppercorns in brine

22ml/1½ tbsp skimmed milk powder

7.5ml/1½ tsp salt

10ml/2 tsp granulated sugar

7.5ml/1½ tsp easy-blend dried yeast

milk, for brushing (optional)

LARGE

330ml/11½fl oz/1⅜ cups water

45ml/3 tbsp extra virgin olive oil

225g/8oz/1⅓ cups canned chickpeas

675g/1½lb/6 cups unbleached white bread flour

15ml/1 tbsp drained fresh pink peppercorns in brine

15ml/1 tbsp drained fresh green peppercorns in brine

30ml/2 tbsp skimmed milk powder

10ml/2 tsp salt

15ml/1 tbsp granulated sugar

7.5ml/1½ tsp easy-blend dried yeast

milk, for brushing (optional)

MAKES 1 LOAF

1 Pour the water and extra virgin olive oil into the bread machine pan. Add the well-drained chickpeas. If the instructions for your bread machine specify that the yeast is to be placed in the pan first, then simply reverse the order in which you add the liquid and dry ingredients to the bread pan.

2 Sprinkle over the flour, ensuring that it covers the ingredients already placed in the pan. Add the pink and green peppercorns and milk powder.

3 Place the salt and sugar in separate corners of the pan. Make a small indent in the centre of the flour (but not down as far as the liquid) and add the yeast.

4 Set the bread machine to the basic/normal setting, medium crust. Press Start. If you like, brush the top of the loaf with milk just before the bread starts to bake.

5 Remove the bread at the end of the baking cycle and turn out on to a wire rack to cool.

BELOW: A peel is useful when making pizzas

Springform cake tins (pans) with diameters of 20–25cm/8–10in make the removal of sweet breads and cakes much easier than when a fixed-based cake tin is used. Square and rectangular tins are perfect for sweet- and savoury-topped breads.

Focaccia or deep-pan pizzas are best cooked in a large, shallow, round cake tin with a diameter of 25–28cm/ 10–11in. A fluted loose-based tart pan and shallow pizza pan are good investments if you cook those types of bread regularly.

Shaped moulds are often used for baking speciality breads. A fluted mould with sloping sides is the classic shape for both individual and large Brioche. Kugelhopf is made in a deep fluted tin with a central hole, Savarin in a shallow ring mould and Babas in shallow, individual ring moulds.

FRENCH BAGUETTE TRAY

A moulded tray, designed to hold two or three loaves, this has a perforated base to ensure an even heat while baking. The bread is given its final proving in the tray, which is then placed in the oven for baking. Loaves baked in a tray will have small dimples on the base and sides.

BAKING SHEETS

A number of free-form breads need to be transferred to a baking sheet for cooking. A selection of strong, heavy baking sheets is best. Use either totally flat baking sheets, or ones with a lip on one edge only. These make it possible to remove the cooked breads easily.

BAKING STONE

For more rustic bread, sourdoughs, pizza and focaccia, a baking stone or pizza stone helps to ensure a crisp crust.

TERRACOTTA TILES

Unglazed quarry tiles or terracotta tiles can be used instead of a baking stone. The tiles will draw out moisture and help to produce the traditional crisp crust.

PEEL

If you are regularly going to use a baking stone or tiles, a peel (baker's shovel) is a useful piece of equipment. Use it to slide pizzas and bread doughs into the oven, placing them directly on to the preheated surface. Flour the peel generously and place the bread on it for its final proving. Give it a gentle shake just before placing it in the oven to make sure the base of the bread doesn't stick to the peel.

WATER SPRAY BOTTLE

Use a water spray bottle to mist the oven when you wish to achieve a crisp crust. A pump-action plastic bottle with a fine spray-head is ideal.

USEFUL TOOLS

This section includes tools for preparing ingredients and for finishing hand-shaped and machine breads.

CUTTERS

Plain cutters are used to cut dough for muffins and rolls. Metal cutters are best as they are not distorted when pressure is applied. A range of cutters 5–10cm/ 2–4in in diameter is most useful.

POTATO PEELER

Use a fixed-blade potato peeler for peeling vegetables and fruit, or removing strips of citrus peel. A swivel-blade peeler is useful for paring very thin layers of citrus skin.

ZESTER

Many sweet breads and cakes include fresh citrus zest and this handy little tool makes light work of preparing it. The zester has a row of holes with cutting edges which shave off thin strips of zest without including the bitter pith that lies just beneath the coloured citrus peel. You may then wish to chop the strips into smaller pieces with a very sharp knife.

PASTRY BRUSHES

These are used to apply washes and glazes. Avoid nylon brushes, which will melt if used on hot breads. Brushes made from natural fibre are better.

LEFT: A baking stone, terracotta tiles and a water spray all help to produce breads with a crispier crust.

VEGETABLE BREADS

The subtle orange hue from pumpkin or carrot, the orangey-red crumb from tomatoes and the amazing colours of spinach or beetroot bread are only part of the story. Vegetables – grated, puréed, mashed or chopped – can be incorporated into bread doughs to provide wonderfully flavoured and coloured loaves. Almost any vegetable can be used, often in conjunction with spices, as in Carrot and Fennel Bread, or seeds, as in Courgette Country Grain Bread.

Plastic Scraper and Spatula

Make sure these tools are pliable. Use them to help remove dough that is stuck on the inside of the bread machine pan. The scraper also comes in handy for lifting and turning sticky dough and dividing dough into pieces for shaping into rolls.

Knives

You will need a sharp cook's knife for slashing doughs and a smaller paring knife for preparing fruit and vegetables.

Scissors and Scalpel

Both these items can be used for slashing breads and rolls, to give decorative finishes before baking. A medium-size pair of scissors with thin, pointed blades is perfect. If you use a scalpel, replace the blade regularly, as it must be sharp.

Rolling Pins

Some breads and buns need to be rolled out for shaping. Cylindrical wooden pins are best. Use a heavy rolling pin about 45cm/18in long for breads and a smaller one for individual rolls, buns and pastries. A child's toy rolling pin can be useful for fiddly items.

LEFT: Selection of rolling pins

ABOVE: From left to right: spatula, cook's knife, vegetable knife, scalpel and scissors

Thermometers

All ovens cook with slightly different heat intensities. An oven thermometer will enable you to establish how your oven cooks so you can adjust recipes. The time-honoured way of testing if a loaf is cooked through is to tap it on the base to see if it sounds hollow.

A much more scientific method is to insert a thermometer into the centre of a hand-shaped loaf and check the internal temperature. It should be 190–195°C (375–383°F).

Sieves

A large sieve is essential for sifting flours together, and small sieves are useful for sifting ingredients such as dried skimmed milk (non fat dry milk), icing (confectioner's) sugar and ground spices. Use a plastic sieve for icing sugar, so as not to discolour the sugar.

COOLING AND SLICING

Cooling a bread properly gives a crispier crust. The bread is then ready to eat.

Oven Gloves

A thick pair of oven gloves or mitts is essential for lifting the bread pan from the machine or breads from the oven, because the metal items will be very hot.

Wire Rack

The hot cooked bread should be turned out on to a wire rack and left to cool before storing or slicing.

Bread Knife and Board

To preserve the delicate crumb structure, bread should be sawn with a sharp knife that has a long serrated blade. Cut the bread on a wooden board to prevent damaging the serrated knife.

ABOVE: Oven gloves, and a wire rack for cooling bread

GARLIC AND HERB WALNUT BREAD

Walnut bread is very popular in France. This variation includes both garlic and basil for additional flavour.

SMALL
150ml/5fl oz/⅔ cup milk
60ml/2fl oz/4 tbsp water
30ml/2 tbsp extra virgin olive oil
325g/11½oz/scant 3 cups unbleached white bread flour
40g/1½oz/scant ⅓ cup rolled oats
40g/1½oz/⅓ cup chopped walnuts
1 garlic clove, finely chopped
5ml/1 tsp dried oregano
5ml/1 tsp drained fresh basil in sunflower oil
5ml/1 tsp salt
7.5ml/1½ tsp granulated sugar
2.5ml/½ tsp easy-blend (rapid-rise) dried yeast

MEDIUM
185ml/6½fl oz/generous ¾ cup milk
105ml/7 tbsp water
45ml/3 tbsp extra virgin olive oil
450g/1lb/4 cups unbleached white bread flour
50g/2oz/½ cup rolled oats
50g/2oz/½ cup chopped walnuts
1½ garlic cloves, finely chopped
7.5ml/1½ tsp dried oregano
7.5ml/1½ tsp drained fresh basil in sunflower oil
7.5ml/1½ tsp salt
10ml/2 tsp granulated sugar
5ml/1 tsp easy-blend dried yeast

LARGE
200ml/7fl oz/scant 1 cup milk
140ml/5fl oz/⅔ cup water
60ml/4 tbsp extra virgin olive oil
600g/1lb 5oz/generous 5¼ cups unbleached white bread flour
65g/2½oz/scant ⅔ cup rolled oats
65g/2½oz/generous ½ cup chopped walnuts
2 garlic cloves, finely chopped
7.5ml/1½ tsp dried oregano
7.5ml/1½ tsp drained fresh basil in sunflower oil
10ml/2 tsp salt
10ml/2 tsp granulated sugar
7.5ml/1½ tsp easy-blend dried yeast

MAKES 1 LOAF

1 Pour the milk, water and olive oil into the bread machine pan. If the instructions for your machine specify that the yeast is to be placed in the pan first, reverse the order in which you add the liquid and dry ingredients.

2 Sprinkle over the flour and rolled oats, ensuring that they completely cover the liquid mixture. Add the chopped walnuts, garlic, oregano and basil. Place the salt and sugar in separate corners of the bread machine pan. Make a small indent in the centre of the flour (but do not go down as far as the liquid) and add the easy-blend dried yeast.

3 Set the bread machine to the basic/normal setting, medium crust. Press Start.

4 Remove the bread at the end of the baking cycle and turn out on to a wire rack to cool.

BASIC BREADS

These recipes are the everyday breads that you will want to make time and again. They are some of the easiest breads to make in your machine; perfect for serving toasted with lashings of butter or for use in sandwiches. The range of breads includes wholemeal, Granary and rye breads, and those flavoured and enriched with milk, buttermilk, eggs, potato or rice. If you haven't made bread in your machine before, this is the place to start.

SUN-DRIED TOMATO BREAD

The dense texture and highly concentrated flavour of sun-dried tomatoes makes them perfect for flavouring bread dough, and when Parmesan cheese is added, the result is an exceptionally tasty loaf.

SMALL

15g/½oz/¼ cup sun-dried tomatoes
130ml/4½fl oz/½ cup + 1 tbsp water
70ml/2½fl oz/¼ cup + 1 tbsp milk
15ml/1 tbsp extra virgin olive oil
325g/11½oz/scant 3 cups unbleached
white bread flour
50g/2oz/½ cup wholemeal
(whole-wheat) bread flour
40g/1½oz/½ cup freshly grated
Parmesan cheese
5ml/1 tsp salt
5ml/1 tsp granulated sugar
4ml/¾ tsp easy-blend (rapid-rise)
dried yeast

MEDIUM

25g/1oz/½ cup sun-dried tomatoes
190ml/6¾fl oz/scant ⅞ cup water
115ml/4fl oz/½ cup milk
30ml/2 tbsp extra virgin olive oil
425g/15oz/3¾ cups unbleached white
bread flour
75g/3oz/¾ cup wholemeal bread flour
50g/2oz/⅔ cup freshly grated
Parmesan cheese
7.5ml/1½ tsp salt
10ml/2 tsp granulated sugar
5ml/1 tsp easy-blend dried yeast

LARGE

40g/1½oz/¾ cup sun-dried tomatoes
240ml/8½fl oz/generous 1 cup water
140ml/5fl oz/⅝ cup milk
45ml/3 tbsp extra virgin olive oil
575g/1¼lb/5 cups unbleached white
bread flour
100g/4oz/1 cup wholemeal bread flour
75g/3oz/1 cup freshly grated
Parmesan cheese
10ml/2 tsp salt
10ml/2 tsp granulated sugar
7.5ml/1½ tsp easy-blend dried yeast

MAKES 1 LOAF

1 Place the sun-dried tomatoes in a small bowl and pour over enough warm water to cover them. Leave to soak for 15 minutes, then tip into a sieve placed over a bowl. Allow to drain thoroughly, then chop finely.

2 Check the quantity of tomato water against the amount of water required for the loaf, and add more water if this is necessary. Pour it into the bread machine pan, then add the milk and olive oil. If the instructions for your machine specify that the yeast is to be placed in the pan first, then simply reverse the order in which you add the liquid and dry ingredients.

3 Sprinkle over both types of flour, ensuring that the liquid is completely covered. Sprinkle over the Parmesan, then add the salt and sugar, placing them in separate corners of the bread pan. Make a small indent in the centre of the flour (but not down as far as the liquid) and add the yeast.

4 Set the bread machine to the basic/normal setting; use raisin setting (if available), medium crust. Press Start. Add the tomatoes at the beep or during the last 5 minutes of kneading. Remove the bread at the end of the baking cycle and turn out on to a wire rack to cool.

RAPID WHITE BREAD

A delicious basic white loaf which can be cooked on the fastest setting.
It is the ideal bread if you are in a hurry.

SMALL
210ml/7½fl oz/scant 1 cup water
22ml/1½ tbsp sunflower oil
375g/13oz/3¼ cups unbleached white
bread flour
15ml/1 tbsp skimmed milk powder
(non fat dry milk)
7.5ml/1½ tsp salt
15ml/1 tbsp granulated sugar
5ml/1 tsp easy-blend (rapid-rise)
dried yeast

MEDIUM
315ml/11fl oz/1⅓ cups water
30ml/2 tbsp sunflower oil
500g/1lb 2oz/4½ cups unbleached
white bread flour
22ml/1½ tbsp skimmed milk powder
7.5ml/1½ tsp salt
22ml/1½ tbsp granulated sugar
7.5ml/1½ tsp easy-blend dried yeast

LARGE
420ml/15fl oz/generous 1¾
cups water
45ml/3 tbsp sunflower oil
675g/1½lb/6 cups unbleached white
bread flour
30ml/2 tbsp skimmed milk powder
10ml/2 tsp salt
30ml/2 tbsp granulated sugar
10ml/2 tsp easy-blend dried yeast

MAKES 1 LOAF

1 Pour the water and the sunflower oil into the bread machine pan. However, if the instructions for your particular machine specify that the yeast is to be placed in the pan first, then reverse the order in which you add the liquid and dry ingredients.

2 Sprinkle over the flour, covering the water. Add the milk powder. Place the salt and sugar in separate corners of the bread pan. Make a shallow indent in the centre of the flour (but not down as far as the liquid) and add the yeast.

3 Set the bread machine to the rapid/quick setting, medium crust. Press Start.

4 Remove the bread at the end of the baking cycle and turn out on to a wire rack to cool.

COOK'S TIP
On the quick setting the yeast has less time to work, and breads may not rise as high as those cooked on the basic/normal setting.
In cold weather it may be necessary to use lukewarm water, to help speed up the action of the yeast.

Basic Breads

ROSEMARY AND RAISIN LOAF

Inspired by a classic Tuscan bread – panmarino – this bread is flavoured with rosemary and raisins and enriched with eggs and olive oil.

1 Pour the water, extra virgin olive oil and egg(s) into the bread machine pan. If the instructions for your machine specify that the yeast is to be placed in the pan first, then simply reverse the order in which you add the liquid and dry ingredients.

2 Sprinkle over the flour, ensuring that it covers the water. Add the skimmed milk powder and rosemary. Add the salt and sugar in separate corners of the bread pan. Make a small indent in the centre of the flour (but not down as far as the liquid) and add the yeast.

3 Set the bread machine to the basic/normal setting, with raisin setting (if available), medium crust. Press Start. Add the raisins when the machine beeps or 5 minutes before the kneading cycle ends.

4 Remove the bread at the end of the baking cycle and turn out on to a wire rack to cool.

SMALL
135ml/4½fl oz/scant ⅔ cup water
45ml/3 tbsp extra virgin olive oil
1 egg
375g/13oz/3¼ cups unbleached white bread flour
15ml/1 tbsp skimmed milk powder (non fat dry milk)
10ml/2 tsp fresh rosemary, chopped
5ml/1 tsp salt
10ml/2 tsp granulated sugar
5ml/1 tsp easy-blend (rapid-rise) dried yeast
75g/3oz/½cup raisins

MEDIUM
160ml/5½fl oz/generous ⅔ cup water
60ml/4 tbsp extra virgin olive oil
2 eggs
500g/1lb 2oz/4½ cups unbleached white bread flour
30ml/2 tbsp skimmed milk powder
15ml/1 tbsp fresh rosemary, chopped
7.5ml/1½ tsp salt
10ml/2 tsp granulated sugar
5ml/1 tsp easy-blend dried yeast
115g/4oz/generous ⅔ cup raisins

LARGE
200ml/7fl oz/⅞ cup water
75ml/5 tbsp extra virgin olive oil
3 eggs
675g/1½lb/6 cups unbleached white bread flour
45ml/3 tbsp skimmed milk powder
20ml/4 tsp fresh rosemary, chopped
7.5ml/1½ tsp salt
15ml/1 tbsp granulated sugar
7.5ml/1½ tsp easy-blend dried yeast
150g/5oz/1 cup raisins

MAKES 1 LOAF

VARIATION
This savoury bread can be made with chopped almonds and sultanas (golden raisins) or dried figs, instead of raisins. All are delicious flavours for serving with soft cheese.

Milk Loaf

Adding milk results in a soft, velvety grained loaf with a beautifully browned crust. Milk also improves the keeping quality of the bread.

SMALL
180ml/6½fl oz/generous ¾ cup milk
60ml/2fl oz/¼ cup water
375g/13oz/3¼ cups unbleached white
bread flour
7.5ml/1½ tsp salt
10ml/2 tsp granulated sugar
20g/¾oz/1½ tbsp butter
2.5ml/½ tsp easy-blend (rapid-rise)
dried yeast

MEDIUM
200ml/7fl oz/⅞ cup milk
100ml/3½fl oz/7 tbsp water
450g/1lb/4 cups unbleached white
bread flour
7.5ml/1½ tsp salt
10ml/2 tsp granulated sugar
25g/1oz/2 tbsp butter
5ml/1 tsp easy-blend dried yeast

LARGE
280ml/10fl oz/1¼ cups milk
130ml/4½fl oz/½ cup + 1 tbsp water
675g/1½lb/6 cups unbleached white
bread flour
10ml/2 tsp salt
15ml/1 tbsp granulated sugar
25g/1oz/2 tbsp butter
7.5ml/1½ tsp easy-blend dried yeast

MAKES 1 LOAF

COOK'S TIP
The milk should be at room
temperature, or it will retard the
action of the yeast and the bread will
not rise properly. Remove the milk
from the refrigerator 30 minutes
before use. You can use full-cream
(whole) or semi-skimmed (low-fat) milk.

1 Pour the milk and water into the bread machine pan. If the instructions for your machine specify that the yeast is to be placed in the pan first, reverse the order in which you add the liquid and dry ingredients.

2 Sprinkle over the flour, ensuring that it covers the water. Add the salt, sugar and butter in separate corners of the bread pan. Make a small indent in the centre of the flour (but not down as far as the liquid) and add the yeast.

3 Set the bread machine to the basic/normal setting, medium crust. Press Start.

4 Remove the bread at the end of the baking cycle and turn out on to a wire rack to cool.

POPPY SEED LOAF

Poppy seeds are popular in Eastern European breads. They have a mild, sweet, slightly nutty flavour and make an interesting addition to this loaf.

SMALL
180ml/6½fl oz/generous ¾ cup milk
60ml/2fl oz/¼ cup water
375g/13oz/3¼ cups unbleached white
bread flour
45ml/3 tbsp poppy seeds
7.5ml/1½ tsp salt
10ml/2 tsp granulated sugar
20g/¾oz/1½ tbsp butter
5ml/1 tsp easy-blend (rapid-rise)
dried yeast

MEDIUM
200ml/7fl oz/⅞ cup milk
100ml/3½fl oz/7 tbsp water
450g/1lb/4 cups unbleached white
bread flour
60ml/4 tbsp poppy seeds
7.5ml/1½ tsp salt
10ml/2 tsp granulated sugar
25g/1oz/2 tbsp butter
5ml/1 tsp easy-blend dried yeast

LARGE
280ml/10fl oz/1¼ cup milk
130ml/4½fl oz/generous ½ cup water
675g/1½lb/6 cups unbleached white
bread flour
75ml/5 tbsp poppy seeds
10ml/2 tsp salt
15ml/1 tbsp granulated sugar
25g/1oz/2 tbsp butter
7.5ml/1½ tsp easy-blend dried yeast

FOR THE GLAZE (OPTIONAL)
½ egg white
5ml/1 tsp water

MAKES 1 LOAF

1 Pour the milk and water into the bread machine pan. If the instructions for your machine specify that the yeast is to be placed in the pan first, reverse the order in which you add the liquid and dry ingredients.

2 Sprinkle over the flour, ensuring that it covers the water. Add the poppy seeds. Add the salt, sugar and butter in separate corners of the bread pan. Make a small indent in the centre of the flour (but not down as far as the liquid) and add the yeast.

3 Set the bread machine to the basic/normal setting, medium crust. Press Start.

4 If glazing, mix the egg white and water and brush over the loaf just before the baking cycle starts.

5 Remove the bread at the end of the baking cycle and turn out on to a wire rack to cool.

COOK'S TIP
To ensure the poppy seeds stay whole, add them when the machine beeps, or during the last 5 minutes of kneading.

WHITE BREAD

This is a simple all-purpose white bread recipe, which makes the perfect basis for experimenting. Try using different brands of flours and be prepared to make minor alterations to quantities if necessary, to find the optimum recipe for your machine.

SMALL
210ml/7½fl oz/scant 1 cup water
375g/13oz/3¼ cups unbleached white bread flour
7.5ml/1½ tsp salt
15ml/1 tbsp granulated sugar
25g/1oz/2 tbsp butter
5ml/1 tsp easy-blend (rapid-rise) dried yeast
unbleached white bread flour, for dusting

MEDIUM
320ml/11¼fl oz/generous 1⅓ cups water
500g/1lb 2oz/4½ cups unbleached white bread flour
7.5ml/1½ tsp salt
15ml/1 tbsp granulated sugar
25g/1oz/2 tbsp butter
5ml/1 tsp easy-blend dried yeast
unbleached white bread flour, for dusting

LARGE
420ml/15fl oz/generous 1¾ cups water
675g/1½lb/6 cups unbleached white bread flour
10ml/2 tsp salt
22ml/1½ tbsp granulated sugar
40g/1½oz/3 tbsp butter
7.5ml/1½ tsp easy-blend dried yeast
unbleached white bread flour, for dusting

MAKES 1 LOAF

1 Pour the water into the bread machine pan. However, if the instructions for your machine specify that the yeast is to be placed in the pan first, reverse the order in which you add the liquid and dry ingredients.

2 Sprinkle over the flour, ensuring that it covers the water. Add the salt, sugar and butter in separate corners of the bread pan. Make a small indent in the centre of the flour (but not down as far as the liquid) and add the yeast.

COOK'S TIP
To give the crust a richer golden appearance, add skimmed milk powder (non fat dry milk) to the flour. For a small loaf, you will need 15ml/ 1 tbsp; for a medium loaf 22ml/1½ tbsp and for a large loaf 30ml/2 tbsp.

3 Set the bread machine to the basic/normal setting, medium crust. Press Start.

4 Remove the bread at the end of the baking cycle and turn out on to a wire rack to cool.

Basic Breads
59

COTTAGE CHEESE–PEPPERONI LOAF

Cottage cheese gives this bread an interesting texture. It is quite filling, and has a delicious, spicy taste, thanks to the pepperoni and oregano. Serve it with vegetable soups or salad.

1 Place the cottage cheese in the bread machine pan and pour in the water and extra virgin olive oil. If the instructions for your machine specify that the easy-blend dried yeast is to be placed in the bread pan first, then simply reverse the order in which you add the liquid and dry ingredients.

2 Sprinkle over the flour, ensuring that it covers the water. Add the oregano. Add the salt and sugar in separate corners of the bread pan. Make a small indent in the centre of the flour (but not down as far as the liquid) and add the easy-blend dried yeast.

3 Set the bread machine to the basic/normal setting, with raisin setting (if available), medium crust. Press Start. Add the pepperoni and spring onion when the machine beeps or sprinkle them over the dough 5 minutes before the end of the kneading cycle.

4 Remove the bread at the end of the baking cycle and turn out on to a wire rack to cool.

SMALL
100g/3½oz/scant ½ cup cottage cheese
160ml/5½fl oz/generous ⅔ cup water
15ml/1 tbsp extra virgin olive oil
375g/13oz/3¼ cups unbleached white bread flour
5ml/1 tsp dried oregano
5ml/1 tsp salt
7.5ml/1½ tsp granulated sugar
5ml/1 tsp easy-blend (rapid-rise) dried yeast
25g/1oz pepperoni, cut into 5mm/¼in chunks
1 spring onion (scallion), chopped

MEDIUM
170g/6oz/¾ cup cottage cheese
210ml/7½fl oz/scant 1 cup water
22ml/1½ tbsp extra virgin olive oil
500g/1lb 2oz/4½ cups unbleached white bread flour
7.5ml/1½ tsp dried oregano
5ml/1 tsp salt
10ml/2 tsp granulated sugar
7.5ml/1½ tsp easy-blend dried yeast
50g/2oz pepperoni, cut into 5mm/¼in chunks
2 spring onions, chopped

LARGE
225g/8oz/1 cup cottage cheese
280ml/10fl oz/1¼ cups water
30ml/2 tbsp extra virgin olive oil
675g/1½lb/6 cups unbleached white bread flour
10ml/2 tsp dried oregano
7.5ml/1½ tsp salt
15ml/1 tbsp granulated sugar
7.5ml/1½ tsp easy-blend dried yeast
75g/3oz pepperoni, cut into 5mm/¼in chunks
3 spring onions, chopped

MAKES 1 LOAF

COOK'S TIP
Extra ingredients are usually added towards the end of the kneading cycle, and some machines will alert you to this by means of a beep or buzzing noise. Consult the handbook for your machine if necessary.

EGG-ENRICHED WHITE LOAF

Adding egg to a basic white loaf gives a richer flavour and creamier crumb, as well as a golden finish to the crust.

1 Put the egg(s) in a measuring jug (cup) and add sufficient water to give 240ml/8½fl oz/generous 1 cup, 300ml/10½fl oz/1⅓ cups or 430ml/15fl oz/scant 1⅞ cups, according to the size of loaf selected.

2 Mix lightly and pour into the bread machine pan. If your instructions specify that the yeast is to be placed in the pan first, reverse the order in which you add the liquid and the dry ingredients.

SMALL
1 egg
water, see method
375g/13oz/3¼ cups unbleached white bread flour
7.5ml/1½ tsp granulated sugar
7.5ml/1½ tsp salt
20g/¾oz/1½ tbsp butter
4ml/¾ tsp easy-blend (rapid-rise) dried yeast

MEDIUM
1 egg plus 1 egg yolk
water, see method
500g/1lb 2oz/4½ cups unbleached white bread flour
10ml/2 tsp granulated sugar
7.5ml/1½ tsp salt
25g/1oz/2 tbsp butter
5ml/1 tsp easy-blend dried yeast

LARGE
2 eggs
water, see method
675g/1½lb/6 cups unbleached white bread flour
15ml/1 tbsp granulated sugar
10ml/2 tsp salt
25g/1oz/2 tbsp butter
7.5ml/1½ tsp easy-blend dried yeast

MAKES 1 LOAF

3 Sprinkle over the flour, covering the water. Add the sugar, salt and butter in separate corners of the pan. Make a small indent in the centre of the flour and add the yeast.

4 Set the machine to the basic/normal setting, medium crust. Press Start. At the end of the baking cycle, turn out on to a wire rack to cool.

GRAINY MUSTARD AND BEER LOAF

For a ploughman's lunch par excellence, serve chunks of this wonderful bread with cheese and pickles.

COOK'S TIP

Use pale ale for a more subtle taste or brown ale if you prefer a stronger flavour to your bread. Open at least 1 hour before using, to make sure it is flat.

1 Pour the beer and oil into the bread machine pan. Add the mustard. If the instructions for your machine specify that the yeast is to be placed in the pan first, reverse the order in which you add the liquid and dry ingredients.

2 Sprinkle over the white and wholemeal flours, ensuring that the liquid is completely covered. Add the skimmed milk powder. Add the salt and sugar, placing them in separate corners of the bread pan. Make a small indent in the centre of the flour (but not down as far as the liquid) and add the yeast.

3 Set the bread machine to the basic/normal setting, medium crust. Press Start.

4 Remove the bread at the end of the baking cycle and turn out on to a wire rack to cool.

Buttermilk Bread

Buttermilk adds a pleasant, slightly sour note to the flavour of this bread. It also gives the bread a good light texture and a golden brown crust. Buttermilk bread tastes especially delicious when toasted and simply spread with a little good quality butter.

SMALL

230ml/8fl oz/1 cup buttermilk
30ml/2 tbsp water
15ml/1 tbsp clear honey
15ml/1 tbsp sunflower oil
250g/9oz/2¼ cups unbleached white bread flour
125g/4½oz/generous 1 cup wholemeal (whole-wheat) bread flour
7.5ml/1½ tsp salt
5ml/1 tsp easy-blend (rapid-rise) dried yeast

MEDIUM

285ml/10fl oz/1¼ cups buttermilk
65ml/4½ tbsp water
22ml/1½ tbsp clear honey
22ml/1½ tbsp sunflower oil
350g/12oz/3 cups unbleached white bread flour
150g/5½oz/1⅓ cup wholemeal bread flour
7.5ml/1½ tsp salt
7.5ml/1½ tsp easy-blend dried yeast

LARGE

370ml/13fl oz/scant 1⅝ cups buttermilk
80ml/5½ tbsp water
30ml/2 tbsp clear honey
30ml/2 tbsp sunflower oil
475g/1lb 1oz/4⅓ cups unbleached white bread flour
200g/7oz/1¾ cups wholemeal bread flour
10ml/2 tsp salt
10ml/2 tsp easy-blend dried yeast

MAKES 1 LOAF

COOK'S TIP

Buttermilk is a by-product of butter making and is the fairly thin liquid left after the fat has been made into butter. It is pasteurized and mixed with a special culture which causes it to ferment, resulting in the characteristic slightly sour flavour. If you run short of buttermilk, using a low-fat natural (plain) yogurt and 5–10ml/1–2 tsp lemon juice is an acceptable alternative.

1 Pour the buttermilk, water, honey and oil into the bread machine pan. If your instructions specify that the yeast is to be placed in the pan first, reverse the order of the liquid and dry ingredients.

2 Sprinkle over both the white and wholemeal flours, ensuring that the water is completely covered. Add the salt in one corner of the bread pan. Make a small indent in the centre of the flour (but not down as far as the liquid) and add the yeast.

3 Set the bread machine to the basic/normal setting, medium crust. Press Start.

4 Remove the bread from the pan at the end of the baking cycle and turn out on to a wire rack to cool.

SAVOURY BREADS

Adding flavourings to a basic dough provides many new ideas. Herbs, such as rosemary, dill and sage, along with garlic and onion will fill the kitchen with delicious scents. Cottage cheese and feta give loaves a subtle flavour, while Gorgonzola, Parmesan and mascarpone are combined with chives to give a rich loaf with a wonderful aroma. Sausages, smoked venison, salami and pancetta are just a few of the meats you can add to savoury breads.

LIGHT WHOLEMEAL BREAD

A tasty, light wholemeal loaf which can be cooked on the quicker basic or normal setting.

SMALL
280ml/10fl oz/1¼ cups water
250g/9oz/2¼ cups wholemeal
(whole-wheat) bread flour
125g/4½oz/generous 1 cup white
bread flour
7.5ml/1½ tsp salt
7.5ml/1½ tsp granulated sugar
20g/¾oz/1½ tbsp butter
5ml/1 tsp easy-blend (rapid-rise)
dried yeast

MEDIUM
350ml/12fl oz/1½ cups water
350g/12oz/3 cups wholemeal bread flour
150g/5½oz/1⅓ cups white bread flour
10ml/2 tsp salt
10ml/2 tsp granulated sugar
25g/1oz/2 tbsp butter
7.5ml/1½ tsp easy-blend dried yeast

LARGE
450ml/16fl oz/scant 2 cups water
475g/1lb 1oz/4¼ cups wholemeal bread flour
200g/7oz/1¾ cups white bread flour
10ml/2 tsp salt
15ml/1 tbsp granulated sugar
25g/1oz/2 tbsp butter
10ml/2 tsp easy-blend dried yeast

MAKES 1 LOAF

VARIATION
This is a fairly light brown loaf as it contains a mixture of white and wholemeal bread flour.
Another option for a lighter brown bread is to replace the wholemeal bread flour with brown bread flour.
This contains less bran and wheatgerm than wholemeal flour, so produces a slightly lighter bread.

1 Pour the water into the bread machine pan. If the instructions for your bread machine specify that the yeast is to be placed in the pan first, reverse the order in which you add the liquid and dry ingredients to the pan.

2 Sprinkle over each type of flour in turn, ensuring that the water is completely covered. Add the salt, sugar and butter in separate corners of the bread pan. Make a small indent in the centre of the flour and add the yeast.

3 Set the bread machine to the basic/normal setting, medium crust. Press Start.

4 Remove the bread at the end of the baking cycle and turn out on to a wire rack to cool.

CHALLAH

The flavour of this traditional Jewish festival bread is enhanced by the use of a sponge starter, which is left to develop for 8–10 hours before the final dough is made. The dough is often braided, but can also be shaped into a coil. This shape is favoured for Jewish New Year celebrations, and symbolizes continuity and eternity.

FOR THE SPONGE
200ml/7fl oz/⅞ cup water
225g/8oz/2 cups unbleached white bread flour
15ml/1 tbsp granulated sugar
5ml/1 tsp salt
7.5ml/1½ tsp easy-blend (rapid-rise) dried yeast

FOR THE DOUGH
2 eggs
225g/8oz/2 cups unbleached white bread flour
15ml/1 tbsp granulated sugar
5ml/1 tsp salt
50g/2oz/¼ cup butter, melted

FOR THE TOPPING
1 egg yolk
15ml/1 tbsp water
poppy seeds

MAKES 1 LOAF

1 Pour the water for the sponge into the bread machine pan. Reverse the order in which you add the wet and dry ingredients if necessary.

2 Sprinkle over the flour ensuring that it covers the water. Add the sugar and salt in separate corners. Make an indent in the centre of the flour and add the yeast.

3 Set the bread machine to the dough setting; use basic dough setting (if available). Press Start.

4 When the dough cycle has finished, switch the machine off, leaving the sponge inside. Do not lift the lid. Leave the sponge in the machine for 8 hours. If necessary, transfer to a bowl, cover with a damp dishtowel and set aside.

5 Remove the bread pan from the machine and replace the sponge (if necessary). Add the eggs for the dough to the sponge. Sprinkle over the flour. Place the sugar, salt and melted butter in separate corners of the bread pan. Set the bread machine to the dough setting; use basic dough setting (if available). Press Start. Lightly oil a baking sheet.

6 When the dough cycle has finished, remove the dough from the machine and place it on a lightly floured surface. Knock it back (punch it down) gently, then flatten the dough until it is about 2.5cm/ 1in thick. Fold both sides to the centre, fold the dough over again and press to seal.

7 Using your palms, gradually roll the dough into a rope with tapered ends. It should be about 50cm/20in long. Coil the rope into a spiral shape, sealing the final end by tucking it under the loaf. Place the coil on the prepared baking sheet. Cover it with a large glass bowl or lightly oiled clear film (plastic wrap) and leave in a warm place for 45–60 minutes, or until almost doubled in size.

8 Preheat the oven to 190°C/375°F/ Gas 5. In a small bowl, beat the egg yolk with the water for the topping. Brush the mixture over the challah. Sprinkle evenly with the poppy seeds and bake for 35–40 minutes, or until the bread is a deep golden brown and sounds hollow when tapped on the base. Transfer it to a wire rack to cool before slicing.

CORN MEAL BREAD

This scrumptuous bread has a sweet flavour and crumbly texture.
Use a finely ground meal from the health-food store. The coarsely ground
meal used for polenta makes a good topping.

SMALL

150ml/5fl oz/⅔ cup water
75ml/2½fl oz/5 tbsp milk
15ml/1 tbsp corn oil
275g/10oz/2½ cups unbleached white
bread flour
100g/3½oz/scant 1 cup corn meal
5ml/1 tsp salt
7.5ml/1½ tsp light muscovado
(brown) sugar
5ml/1 tsp easy-blend (rapid-rise)
dried yeast
water, for glazing
polenta, for sprinkling

MEDIUM

210ml/7½fl oz/scant 1 cup water
90ml/3fl oz/6 tbsp milk
22ml/1½ tbsp corn oil
350g/12½oz/3 cups unbleached white
bread flour
150g/5oz/1¼ cups corn meal
5ml/1 tsp salt
10ml/2 tsp light muscovado sugar
5ml/1 tsp easy-blend dried yeast
water, for glazing
polenta, for sprinkling

LARGE

250ml/9fl oz/generous 1 cup water
150ml/5fl oz/⅔ cup milk
30ml/2 tbsp corn oil
450g/1lb/4 cups unbleached white
bread flour
225g/8oz/2 cups corn meal
7.5ml/1½ tsp salt
15ml/1 tbsp light muscovado sugar
7.5ml/1½ tsp easy-blend dried yeast
water, for glazing
polenta, for sprinkling

MAKES 1 LOAF

COOK'S TIP

This bread is best cooked on a rapid
setting, even though the inclusion of
corn meal will result in a slightly
shallow loaf. Corn meal, also known as
maize meal, is available from most
health-food stores.

1 Pour the water, milk and corn oil into
the pan. Reverse the order in which you
add the wet and dry ingredients if the
instructions to your machine specify this.

2 Add the flour and the corn meal,
covering the water. Place the salt and
sugar in separate corners. Make a
shallow indent in the flour; add the yeast.

3 Set the bread machine to the rapid/
quick setting, medium crust. Press
Start. Just before the baking cycle
commences brush the top of the loaf
with water and sprinkle with polenta.

4 Remove the bread at the end of the
baking cycle and turn out on to a wire
rack to cool.

SAN FRANCISCO-STYLE SOURDOUGH

This tangy, chewy bread originated in San Francisco, but the flavour will actually be unique to wherever it is baked. The bread is made without baker's yeast, instead using airborne yeast spores to ferment a flour and water paste.

For the Starter
*25g/1oz/¼ cup organic plain
(all-purpose) flour
15–30ml/1–2 tbsp warm water*

*1st Refreshment for the Starter
30ml/2 tbsp water
15ml/1 tbsp milk
50g/2oz/½ cup organic plain flour*

*2nd Refreshment for the Starter
90ml/6 tbsp water
15–30ml/1–2 tbsp milk
175g/6oz/1½ cups organic white
bread flour*

*For the Dough
100ml/3½fl oz/7 tbsp water
175g/6oz/1½ cups organic white
bread flour*

*1st Refreshment for the Dough
100ml/3½fl oz/7 tbsp water
175g/6oz/1½ cups organic white
bread flour
50g/2oz/½ cup organic wholemeal
(whole-wheat) bread flour
7.5ml/1½ tsp salt
5ml/1 tsp granulated sugar
unbleached white bread flour, for
dusting*

Makes 1 Loaf

1 Place the flour in a bowl and stir in enough water for the starter to make a firm, moist dough. Knead for 5 minutes. Cover with a damp cloth. Leave for 2–3 days until a crust forms and the dough inflates with tiny bubbles. Remove the hardened crust and place the moist centre in a clean bowl. Add the water and milk for the 1st refreshment.

2 Gradually add the flour and mix to a firm but moist dough. Cover and leave for 1–2 days as before. Then repeat as for 1st refreshment using the ingredients for the 2nd refreshment. Leave for 8–12 hours in a warm place until well risen.

3 Pour the water for the dough into the pan. Add 200g/7oz/scant 1 cup of starter. If necessary for your machine, add the dry ingredients first. Sprinkle over the flour, covering the water. Set the machine to the dough setting; use basic dough setting (if available). Press Start.

4 Mix for 10 minutes then turn off the machine. Leave the dough in the machine for 8 hours. Add the water for the 1st dough refreshment to the pan, then sprinkle over the flours.

5 Add the salt and sugar in separate corners. Set the machine as before. Press Start. Lightly flour a baking sheet.

6 When the dough cycle ends put the dough on a floured surface. Knock it back (punch it down) gently; shape into a plump ball. Place on the baking sheet; cover with oiled clear film (plastic wrap). Leave for 2 hours, or until almost doubled in bulk.

7 Meanwhile, preheat the oven to 230°C/450°F/Gas 8. Dust the loaf with flour and slash the top in a star shape. Bake for 25 minutes, spraying the oven with water three times in the first 5 minutes. Reduce the oven temperature to 200°C/400°F/Gas 6. Bake the loaf for 10 minutes more or until golden and hollow-sounding. Cool on a wire rack.

ANADAMA BREAD

This traditional New England bread is made with a mixture of white and wholemeal flours and polenta, which is a coarse corn meal. The molasses sweetens the bread and gives it a rich colour.

SMALL
200ml/7fl oz/⅞ cup water
45ml/3 tbsp molasses
5ml/1 tsp lemon juice
275g/10oz/2½ cups unbleached white bread flour
65g/2½oz/generous ½ cup wholemeal (whole-wheat) bread flour
40g/1½oz/⅓ cup polenta
7.5ml/1½ tsp salt
25g/1oz/2 tbsp butter
5ml/1 tsp easy-blend (rapid-rise) dried yeast

MEDIUM
240ml/8½fl oz/generous 1 cup water
60ml/4 tbsp molasses
5ml/1 tsp lemon juice
360g/12½oz/generous 3 cups unbleached white bread flour
75g/3oz/¾ cup wholemeal bread flour
65g/2½oz/generous ½ cup polenta
10ml/2 tsp salt
40g/1½oz/3 tbsp butter
5ml/1 tsp easy-blend dried yeast

LARGE
280ml/10fl oz/1¼ cups water
90ml/5 tbsp molasses
10ml/2 tsp lemon juice
500g/1lb 2oz/4¼ cups unbleached white bread flour
90g/generous 3oz/scant 1 cup wholemeal bread flour
75g/3oz/¾ cup polenta
12.5ml/2½ tsp salt
50g/2oz/¼ cup butter
10ml/2 tsp easy-blend dried yeast

MAKES 1 LOAF

3 Set the bread machine to the basic/normal setting, medium crust. Press Start.

4 Remove the bread at the end of the baking cycle and turn out on to a wire rack to cool.

1 Pour the water, molasses and lemon juice into the bread machine pan. If the instructions for your machine specify that the yeast is to be placed in the pan first, reverse the order in which you add the liquid and dry ingredients.

2 Sprinkle over both types of flour, then the polenta, so that the water is completely covered. Add the salt and butter in separate corners of the bread pan. Make a small indent in the centre of the flour and add the yeast.

CIABATTA

This popular flat loaf is irregularly shaped and typically has large air holes in the crumb. The dough for this bread is extremely wet. Do not be tempted to add more flour – it's meant to be that way.

FOR THE BIGA
200ml/7fl oz/⅞ cup water
*175g/6oz/1½ cups unbleached white
bread flour*
*2.5ml/½ tsp easy-blend (rapid-rise)
dried yeast*

FOR THE CIABATTA DOUGH
200ml/7fl oz/⅞ cup water
30ml/2 tbsp milk
30ml/2 tbsp extra virgin olive oil
*325g/11½oz/scant 3 cups unbleached
white bread flour, plus extra for dusting*
7.5ml/1½ tsp salt
2.5ml/½ tsp granulated sugar
1.5ml/¼ tsp easy-blend dried yeast

MAKES 2 LOAVES

7 Using a spoon or a dough scraper, divide the dough into two portions. Carefully tip one portion of the dough on to one of the prepared baking sheets, trying to avoid knocking the air out of the dough. Using well-floured hands shape the dough into a rectangular loaf about 2.5cm/1in thick, pulling and stretching as necessary. Repeat with the remaining piece of dough.

8 Sprinkle both loaves with flour. Leave them, uncovered, in a warm place for about 20–30 minutes. The dough will spread and rise. Meanwhile, preheat the oven to 220°C/425°F/Gas 7.

9 Bake the ciabatta for 25–30 minutes, or until both loaves have risen, are light golden in colour and sound hollow when tapped on the base. Transfer them to a wire rack to cool before serving with butter, or olive oil for dipping.

1 Pour the water for the biga into the bread pan. If necessary, reverse the order in which you add the liquid and dry ingredients. Sprinkle over the flour, covering the water. Make an indent in the centre of the flour; add the yeast.

2 Set the bread machine to the dough setting; use basic dough setting (if available). Press Start. Mix for 5 minutes, then switch off the machine.

3 Leave the biga in the machine, or place in a large mixing bowl covered with lightly oiled clear film (plastic wrap), overnight or for at least 12 hours, until the dough has risen and is just starting to collapse.

4 Return the biga to the pan, if necessary. Add the water, milk and oil for the ciabatta dough. Sprinkle over the flour. Add the salt and sugar in separate corners. Make a small indent in the centre of the flour and add the yeast.

5 Set the bread machine to the dough setting; use the basic dough setting (if available). Press Start.

6 When the cycle has finished, transfer the dough to a bowl and cover with oiled clear film. Leave to rise for about 1 hour, until the dough has tripled in size. Sprinkle two baking sheets with flour.

FARMHOUSE LOAF

The flour-dusted split top gives a charmingly rustic look to this tasty wholemeal-enriched white loaf.

SMALL
210ml/7½fl oz/scant 1 cup water
350g/12oz/3 cups unbleached white
bread flour, plus extra for dusting
25g/1oz/¼ cup wholemeal
(whole-wheat) bread flour
15ml/1 tbsp skimmed milk powder
(non fat dry milk)
7.5ml/1½ tsp salt
7.5ml/1½ tsp granulated sugar
15g/½oz/1 tbsp butter
4ml/¾ tsp easy-blend (rapid-rise)
dried yeast
water, for glazing

MEDIUM
320ml/11¼fl oz/generous 1⅓ cups water
425g/15oz/3¾ cups unbleached white
bread flour, plus extra for dusting
75g/3oz/¾ cup wholemeal bread flour
22ml/1½ tbsp skimmed milk powder
7.5ml/1½ tsp salt
7.5ml/1½ tsp granulated sugar
25g/1oz/2 tbsp butter
5ml/1 tsp easy-blend dried yeast
water, for glazing

LARGE
420ml/15fl oz/generous 1¾ cups water
600g/1lb 5oz/5¼ cups unbleached white
bread flour, plus extra for dusting
75g/3oz/¾ cup wholemeal bread flour
30ml/2 tbsp skimmed milk powder
10ml/2 tsp salt
10ml/2 tsp granulated sugar
25g/1oz/2 tbsp butter
7.5ml/1½ tsp easy-blend dried yeast
water, for glazing

MAKES 1 LOAF

1 Pour the water into the bread pan. If the instructions for your machine specify that the yeast is to be placed in the pan first, reverse the order in which you add the liquid and dry ingredients. Sprinkle over both the flours, covering the water completely. Add the milk powder. Add the salt, sugar and butter in separate corners. Make an indent in the centre of the flour (but not down as far as the liquid) and add the yeast.

2 Set the bread machine to the basic/normal setting, medium crust. Press Start.

3 Ten minutes before the baking time commences, brush the top of the loaf with water and dust with a little white bread flour. Slash the top of the bread with a sharp knife.

4 Remove the bread at the end of the baking cycle and turn out on to a wire rack to cool.

COOK'S TIP
Try this rustic bread with Granary instead of wholemeal (whole-wheat) bread flour for added texture.

PAIN DE CAMPAGNE

For the Poolish
200ml/7fl oz/⅞ cup water
175g/6oz/1½ cups unbleached white
bread flour
50g/2oz/½ cup wholemeal
(whole-wheat) bread flour
1.5ml/¼ tsp easy-blend (rapid-rise)
dried yeast

For the Dough
120ml/4fl oz/½ cup water
225g/8oz/2 cups unbleached white
bread flour, plus extra for dusting
50g/2oz/½ cup wholemeal bread flour
25g/1oz/¼ cup rye flour
7.5ml/1½ tsp salt
2.5ml/½ tsp granulated sugar
2.5ml/½ tsp easy-blend dried yeast
MAKES 1 LOAF

This rustic-style French bread is made using a poolish or sponge. The fermentation period is fairly short, which makes for a loaf which is not as sour as some breads of this type. It is also lighter and slightly less chewy.

1 Pour the water for the poolish into the bread machine pan. If the instructions for your machine specify that the yeast is to be placed in the pan first, reverse the order in which you add the liquid and dry ingredients.

2 Sprinkle over both types of flour, ensuring that the water is completely covered. Make a small indent in the centre of the flour; add the yeast. Set the bread machine to the dough setting; use basic dough setting (if available). Press Start.

3 When the dough cycle has finished, switch the machine off, but leave the poolish inside, with the lid closed, for 2 – 8 hours, depending on how sour you like your bread to taste.

4 Remove the bread pan from the machine. Pour in the water for the dough. Sprinkle over each type of flour, then add the salt and sugar in separate corners. Make a small indent in the centre of the flour; add the yeast. Set the bread machine to the dough setting. If your machine has a choice of settings, use the basic dough setting. Press Start.

5 When the dough cycle has finished, place the dough on a lightly floured surface. Knock it back (punch it down) gently, then shape it into a plump, round ball. Place on a lightly oiled baking sheet.

6 Cover with a large glass bowl or lightly oiled clear film (plastic wrap) and leave to rise in a warm place for 30–45 minutes, or until almost doubled in bulk. Preheat the oven to 220°C/425°F/Gas 7.

7 Dust the top of the loaf with flour. Cut three parallel slashes across the loaf, then cut three more slashes at right angles to the first set.

8 Transfer the baking sheet to a rack near the bottom of the oven and bake the bread for 40 minutes, or until it is golden and sounds hollow when tapped on the base. Turn out on to a wire rack.

GRANARY BREAD

Granary flour – like Malthouse flour – is a blend, and contains malted wheat grain which gives a crunchy texture to this loaf.

1 Add the water to the bread machine pan. If the instructions for your machine specify that the yeast is to be placed in the pan first, simply reverse the order in which you add the liquid and dry ingredients to the pan.

2 Sprinkle over the flour, ensuring that it covers the water. Add the salt, sugar and butter in separate corners of the bread pan. Make a small indent in the centre of the flour (but not down as far as the liquid) and add the yeast.

3 Set the bread machine to the whole wheat or multi-grain setting, medium crust. Press Start.

4 Remove the bread at the end of the baking cycle and turn out on to a wire rack to cool.

COOK'S TIP
This bread tastes just as good if you use Malthouse bread flour instead of Granary flour.

SMALL
240ml/8½fl oz/generous 1 cup water
375g/13oz/3¼ cups Granary (whole-wheat) bread flour
5ml/1 tsp salt
10ml/2 tsp granulated sugar
20g/¾oz/1½ tbsp butter
2.5ml/½tsp easy-blend (rapid-rise) dried yeast

MEDIUM
350ml/12fl oz/1½ cups water
500g/1lb 2oz/4½ cups Granary bread flour
7.5ml/1½ tsp salt
15ml/1 tbsp granulated sugar
25g/1oz/2 tbsp butter
7.5ml/1½ tsp easy-blend dried yeast

LARGE
400ml/14fl oz/generous 1¾ cups water
675g/1½lb/6 cups Granary bread flour
10ml/2 tsp salt
15ml/1 tbsp granulated sugar
25g/1oz/2 tbsp butter
7.5ml/1½ tsp easy-blend dried yeast

MAKES 1 LOAF

PANE ALL'OLIO

Italians love to use olive oil in cooking, as this bread amply proves.
The combined flavours of the olive oil and the biga starter give a rich,
earthy and yeasty flavour to the bread.

FOR THE BIGA
105ml/7 tbsp water
175g/6oz/1½ cups white bread flour
5ml/1 tsp easy-blend (rapid-rise) dried yeast

FOR THE DOUGH
90ml/6 tbsp water
60ml/4 tbsp extra virgin olive oil
225g/8oz/2 cups unbleached white
bread flour, plus extra for dusting
10ml/2 tsp salt
5ml/1 tsp granulated sugar

MAKES 1 LOAF

COOK'S TIP
If you haven't got a baking stone, you
can use unglazed terracotta tiles.
Place several tiles edge to edge,
ensuring that the air can flow around
the outside edges.

1 Pour the water for the biga into the
bread machine pan. If the instructions
for your machine specify that the yeast
is to be placed in the pan first, reverse
the order in which you add the liquid
and dry ingredients.

2 Sprinkle over the flour, covering the
water. Make a shallow indent in the
centre of the flour and add the yeast.

3 Set the machine to the dough setting;
use basic dough setting (if available).
Press Start.When the dough cycle has
finished, switch the machine off, but
leave the biga inside, with the lid closed,
for 8 hours. If you need the machine
during this time, transfer the biga to a
bowl, cover it with a damp dishtowel
and leave it at room temperature.

4 Remove the bread pan from the
machine. Break the biga into three or
four pieces. If you took it out of the
bread pan, put it back.

5 Pour in the water and olive oil for the
dough. Sprinkle over the flour, covering
the liquid. Add the salt and sugar in
separate corners of the bread pan.

6 Set the bread machine to the dough
setting; use basic dough setting (if
available). Press Start. Lightly flour a
peel (baker's shovel) or baking sheet.

7 When the dough cycle has finished,
place the dough on a lightly floured
surface. Knock it back (punch it down)
gently, then shape it into a plump round.

8 Using the palms of your hands, gently
roll the dough backwards and forwards,
concentrating on the ends, until it forms
a tapered, torpedo-shaped loaf about
30cm/12in long. Place the loaf on the
prepared peel or baking sheet and cover
it with lightly oiled clear film (plastic
wrap). Leave it to rise in a warm place
for 45–60 minutes, or until the dough
has almost doubled in size.

9 Meanwhile, place a baking stone on a
shelf about a third of the way up from
the bottom of the oven. Preheat the
oven to 230°C/450°F/Gas 8. Dust the top
of the bread lightly with flour and slash
it along its length. Transfer the bread to
the hot baking stone.

10 Mist the inside of the oven with
water. Bake the loaf for 15 minutes,
misting the oven again after 2 minutes
and then after 4 minutes. Reduce the
oven temperature to 190°C/375°F/Gas 5
and bake the loaf for 20–25 minutes
more, or until it is golden all over and
the bread sounds hollow when tapped
on the base. Turn out on to a wire rack
before serving warm or cooled.

MALTED LOAF

A malt and sultana loaf makes the perfect breakfast or tea-time treat.
Serve it sliced and generously spread with butter.

SMALL
200ml/7fl oz/⅞ cup water
15ml/1 tbsp golden (light corn) syrup
22ml/1½ tbsp malt extract
350g/12oz/3 cups unbleached white bread flour
22ml/1½ tbsp skimmed milk powder (non fat dry milk)
2.5ml/½ tsp salt
40g/1½oz/3 tbsp butter
2.5ml/½ tsp easy-blend dried (rapid-rise) yeast
75g/3oz/½ cup sultanas (golden raisins)

MEDIUM
280ml/10fl oz/1¼ cups water
22ml/1½ tbsp golden syrup
30ml/2 tbsp malt extract
500g/1lb 2oz/4½ cups unbleached white bread flour
30ml/2 tbsp skimmed milk powder
5ml/1 tsp salt
50g/2oz/¼ cup butter
5ml/1 tsp easy-blend dried yeast
100g/3½oz/generous ½ cup sultanas

LARGE
360ml/scant13fl oz/1½ cups water
30ml/2 tbsp golden syrup
45ml/3 tbsp malt extract
675g/1½lb/6 cups unbleached white bread flour
30ml/2 tbsp skimmed milk powder
5ml/1 tsp salt
65g/2½oz/5 tbsp butter
7.5ml/1½ tsp easy-blend dried yeast
125g/4½oz/generous ⅔ cup sultanas

MAKES 1 LOAF

1 Pour the water, golden syrup and malt extract into the bread machine pan. If the instructions for your machine specify that the yeast is to be placed in the pan first, reverse the order in which you add the liquid and dry ingredients.

2 Sprinkle over the flour so that it covers the liquid. Add the milk powder. Add the salt and butter in separate corners. Make a shallow indent in the centre of the flour and add the yeast.

3 Set the bread machine to the basic/normal setting, with raisin setting (if available), medium crust. Press Start. Add the sultanas when the machine beeps or after the first kneading.

4 Remove at the end and turn out on to a wire rack. If you like, glaze the bread immediately. Dissolve 15ml/1 tbsp caster (superfine) sugar in 15ml/1 tbsp milk and brush over the top crust.

Basic Breads

HONEY AND BEER RYE BREAD

The flavour of this rye bread is enhanced by leaving the sourdough starter to develop over 3 days as a prelude to making the dough.

FOR THE STARTER
175ml/6fl oz/¾ cup milk
115g/4oz/1 cup rye flour
4ml/¾ tsp easy-blend (rapid-rise)
dried yeast

FOR THE DOUGH
170ml/6fl oz/scant ¾ cup flat beer
300g/10½oz/scant 2¾ cups
unbleached white bread flour
85g/3oz/¾ cup rye flour
15ml/1 tbsp clear honey
7.5ml/1½ tsp salt
2.5ml/½ tsp easy-blend dried yeast
wholemeal (whole-wheat) flour,
for dusting
MAKES 1 LOAF

1 Mix the milk, flour and yeast for the starter in a large bowl. Stir, then cover with a damp dishtowel. Rest in a warm place for 3 days; stir once a day.

2 Make the dough. Tip the starter into the bread machine pan and add the beer. If the instructions for your machine specify that the yeast is to be placed in the pan first, simply reverse the order in which you add the liquid and dry ingredients.

3 Sprinkle over both types of flour, ensuring that the beer is completely covered. Add the honey and salt, placing them in separate corners of the bread pan. Make a small indent in the centre of the flour (but not down as far as the liquid) and add the yeast.

4 Set the bread machine to the dough setting; use basic dough setting (if available). Press Start. Lightly oil a 17cm/6½in square tin (pan) that is fairly deep.

5 When the dough cycle has finished, remove the dough from the machine and place it on a lightly floured surface. Knock it back (punch it down) gently.

6 Roll the dough into a rectangle about 2cm/¾in thick. It needs to be the same width as the tin and three times as long. Fold the bottom third of the dough up and the top third down, then seal the edges with the rolling pin.

7 Place the folded dough in the prepared tin, cover it with lightly oiled clear film (plastic wrap) and leave in a warm place for 45–60 minutes, or until the dough has risen almost to the top of the tin.

8 Meanwhile, preheat the oven to 220°C/425°F/Gas 7. Dust the top of the loaf with a little wholemeal flour.

9 Using a sharp knife slash the loaf with four long cuts. Repeat with five cuts in the opposite direction to give a cross-hatched effect.

10 Bake the bread for 30–35 minutes, or until it sounds hollow when tapped on the base. Turn out on to a wire rack to cool slightly before serving.

Sourdoughs & Starter Dough Breads

LIGHT RYE AND CARAWAY BREAD

Rye flour adds a distinctive slightly sour flavour to bread. Rye breads can be dense, so the flour is usually mixed with wheat flour to lighten the texture.

1 Add the water, lemon juice and oil to the bread pan. If your instructions specify that the yeast is to be placed in the pan first, reverse the order in which you add the liquid and dry ingredients.

2 Sprinkle over the rye flour and the white bread flour, ensuring they cover the water. Add the skimmed milk powder and caraway seeds. Add the salt and sugar in separate corners of the bread pan. Make a small indent in the centre of the flour, but not down as far as the liquid, and add the yeast.

3 Set the bread machine to the basic/normal setting, medium crust. Press Start.

4 Remove the bread from the pan at the end of the cycle and transfer to a wire rack to cool.

SMALL

210ml/7½fl oz/scant 1 cup water
5ml/1 tsp lemon juice
15ml/1 tbsp sunflower oil
85g/3oz/¾ cup rye flour
285g/10oz/2½ cups unbleached white bread flour
15ml/1 tbsp skimmed milk powder (non fat dry milk)
5ml/1 tsp caraway seeds
5ml/1 tsp salt
10ml/2 tsp light muscovado (brown) sugar
3.5ml/¾ tsp easy-blend (rapid-rise) dried yeast

MEDIUM

300ml/10½fl oz/1¼ cups water
10ml/2 tsp lemon juice
22ml/1½ tbsp sunflower oil
125g/4½oz/generous 1 cup rye flour
375g/13oz/3¼ cups unbleached white bread flour
22ml/1½ tbsp skimmed milk powder
7.5ml/1½ tsp caraway seeds
7.5ml/1½ tsp salt
15ml/1 tbsp light muscovado sugar
5ml/1 tsp easy-blend dried yeast

LARGE

370ml/13fl oz/scant 1⅝ cups water
10ml/2 tsp lemon juice
30ml/2 tbsp sunflower oil
175g/generous 6oz/generous 1½ cups rye flour
500g/1lb 2oz/4½ cups unbleached white bread flour
30ml/2 tbsp skimmed milk powder
10ml/2 tsp caraway seeds
10ml/2 tsp salt
20ml/4 tsp light muscovado sugar
7.5ml/1½ tsp easy-blend dried yeast

MAKES 1 LOAF

Basic Breads

SCHIACCIATA CON UVA

A Tuscan bread baked to celebrate the grape harvest. The fresh grapes on top are the new crop while the raisins inside symbolize last year's gathering-in.

FOR THE STARTER
200ml/7fl oz/⅞ cup water
175g/6oz/1½ cups organic white
bread flour
1.5ml/¼ tsp easy-blend (rapid-rise)
dried yeast

FOR THE SCHIACCIATA DOUGH
200g/7oz/generous 1 cup raisins
150ml/5fl oz/⅔ cup Italian red wine
45ml/3 tbsp extra virgin olive oil
45ml/3 tbsp water
280g/10oz/2½ cups unbleached white
bread flour
50g/2oz/¼ cup granulated sugar
7.5ml/1½ tsp salt
5ml/1 tsp easy-blend (rapid-rise)
dried yeast

FOR THE TOPPING
280g/10oz small black seedless grapes
30ml/2 tbsp demerara (raw) sugar

MAKES 1 LOAF

1 Pour the water for the starter into the bread machine pan. If the instructions for your machine specify that the yeast is to be placed in the pan first, reverse the order in which you add the liquid and dry ingredients.

2 Sprinkle over the organic flour, ensuring that it completely covers the water. Make a small indent in the centre of the flour (but not down as far as the liquid) and add the easy-blend dried yeast. Set the bread machine to the dough setting; use basic dough setting (if available). Press Start. Mix for 5 minutes, then switch off the machine and set aside.

3 Leave the starter to ferment inside the machine for 24 hours. Do not lift the lid. If you need the machine, transfer the starter to a bowl, cover it with a damp dishtowel and leave it to stand at room temperature.

4 Place the raisins for the dough in a small pan. Add the wine and heat gently until warm. Cover and set aside.

5 Remove the bread pan from the machine. Return the starter to the pan, if necessary, and pour in the oil and water. Sprinkle over the flour. Add the sugar and salt in separate corners. Make a shallow indent in the centre of the flour and add the yeast.

6 Set the bread machine to the dough setting. If your machine has a choice of settings, use the basic dough setting. Press Start. Lightly oil a baking sheet.

7 When the dough cycle has finished, remove the dough from the machine and place it on a lightly floured surface. Knock it back (punch it down) gently, then divide it in half. Roll each piece of dough out into a circle, about 1cm/½in thick. Place one circle on the prepared baking sheet.

8 Spread the raisins over the dough. Place the remaining piece of dough on top and pinch the edges together to seal. Cover with lightly oiled clear film (plastic wrap) and leave to rise in a warm place for 30–45 minutes, or until it is almost doubled in size.

9 Meanwhile, preheat the oven to 190°C/375°F/Gas 5. Cover the schiacciata with the fresh black grapes, pressing them lightly into the dough. Sprinkle with the sugar. Bake for 40 minutes, or until the bread is golden and sounds hollow when tapped on the base. Turn out on to a wire rack to cool slightly before serving.

FRENCH BREAD

French bread traditionally has a crisp crust and light, chewy crumb. Use the special French bread setting on your bread machine to help to achieve this unique texture.

SMALL
MAKES 1 LOAF
150ml/5fl oz/⅔ cup water
225g/8oz/2 cups unbleached white bread flour
5ml/1 tsp salt
7.5ml/1½ tsp easy-blend (rapid-rise) dried yeast

MEDIUM
MAKES 2–3 LOAVES
315ml/11fl oz/1⅓ cups water
450g/1lb/4 cups unbleached white bread flour
7.5ml/1½ tsp salt
7.5ml/1½ tsp easy-blend dried yeast

LARGE
MAKES 3–4 LOAVES
500ml/17½fl oz/2⅛ cups water
675g/1½lb/6 cups unbleached white bread flour
10ml/2 tsp salt
10ml/2 tsp easy-blend dried yeast

1 Add the water to the bread machine pan. If the instructions for your machine specify that the yeast is to be placed in the pan first, reverse the order in which you add the liquid and dry ingredients.

2 Sprinkle over the flour, to cover the water. Add the salt in a corner. Make an indent in the centre of the flour and add the yeast. Use the French bread dough setting (see Cook's Tip). Press Start.

3 When the dough cycle has finished, remove the dough from the machine, place it on a lightly floured surface and knock it back (punch it down). Divide it into two or three equal portions if using the medium quantities or three or four portions if using the large quantities.

4 On a floured surface shape each piece of dough into a ball, then roll out to a rectangle measuring 18–20 × 7.5cm/ 7–8 × 3in. Fold one-third up lengthways and one-third down, then press. Repeat twice more, leaving the dough to rest between foldings to avoid tearing.

5 Gently roll and stretch each piece to a 28–33cm/11–13in loaf, depending on whether you aim to make smaller or larger loaves. Place each loaf in a floured banneton or between the folds of a floured and pleated dishtowel, so that the French bread shape is maintained during rising.

6 Cover with lighly oiled clear film (plastic wrap) and leave in a warm place for 30–45 minutes. Preheat the oven to 230°C/450°F/Gas 8.

7 Roll the loaf or loaves on to a baking sheet, spaced well part. Slash the tops with a knife. Place at the top of the oven, spray the inside of the oven with water and bake for 15–20 minutes, or until golden. Transfer to a wire rack.

COOK'S TIP
Use the French bread baking setting if you do not have a French bread dough setting. Remove the dough before the final rising stage and shape as directed.

FRESH YEAST BREAD

15g/½oz fresh yeast
5ml/1 tsp granulated sugar
260ml/9fl oz/1⅛ cups water
30ml/2 tbsp sunflower oil
450g/1lb/4 cups unbleached white
bread flour
30ml/2 tbsp skimmed milk powder
(non fat dry milk)
10ml/2 tsp salt
75ml/5 tbsp sunflower seeds, for coating

MAKES 1 LOAF

If you particularly like the flavour of fresh yeast, try this recipe. Bread machine manufacturers do not recommend using fresh yeast for bread baked in their appliances, but if the bread is to be baked in the oven, the machine can be used to prepare the dough.

1 In a small bowl, cream the fresh yeast with the sugar and 30ml/2 tbsp of the water. Leave to stand for 5 minutes then scrape the mixture into the bread machine pan. Add the remaining water and the sunflower oil. However, if the instructions for your bread machine specify that the yeast is to be placed in the pan first, simply reverse the order in which you add the liquid and dry ingredients to the pan.

2 Sprinkle over the flour, ensuring that it covers the water completely. Add the skimmed milk powder and salt to the bread pan.

3 Set the bread machine to the dough setting; use basic dough setting (if available). Press Start, then lightly oil a baking sheet.

4 When the dough cycle has finished, remove the dough from the machine and place it on a lightly floured surface. Knock it back (punch it down) gently, and then knead for 2–3 minutes. Roll the dough into a ball and pat it into a plump round cushion shape.

5 Sprinkle the sunflower seeds on a clean area of work surface and roll the bread in them until evenly coated. Place on the prepared baking sheet. Cover with lightly oiled clear film (plastic wrap) or a large inverted bowl and leave to rise in a warm place for 30–45 minutes, or until doubled in size.

6 Meanwhile, preheat the oven to 230°C/450°F/Gas 8. Cut two slashes, one on each side of the loaf, then cut two slashes at right angles to the first to make a noughts and crosses grid.

7 Bake the loaf for 15 minutes, then reduce the oven temperature to 200°C/400°F/Gas 6. Bake for 20 minutes more, or until the bread sounds hollow when tapped on the base. Turn out on to a wire rack to cool.

COOK'S TIP
This makes a basic fresh yeast bread which you can shape or flavour to suit yourself. Leave out the sunflower seeds, if you like.

ITALIAN BREADSTICKS

These crisp breadsticks will keep for a couple of days if stored in an airtight container. If you like, you can refresh them in a hot oven for a few minutes before serving. The dough can be made in any breadmaking machine, regardless of capacity.

200ml/7fl oz/⅞ cup water
45ml/3 tbsp olive oil, plus extra
350g/12oz/3 cups unbleached white bread flour
7.5ml/1½ tsp salt
7.5ml/1½ tsp easy-blend (rapid-rise) dried yeast
poppy seeds and coarse sea salt, for coating (optional)

MAKES 30

COOK'S TIP
If you are rolling the breadsticks in sea salt, don't use too much. Crush the sea salt slightly if the crystals are large.

1 Pour the water and olive oil into the bread machine pan. If the instructions for your machine specify that the yeast is to be placed in the pan first, reverse the order in which you add the liquid and dry ingredients.

2 Sprinkle over the flour, ensuring that it covers the water completely. Add the salt in one corner of the pan. Make a small indent in the centre of the flour (but not down as far as the liquid) and add the easy-blend dried yeast.

3 Set the bread machine to the dough setting; use basic dough setting (if available). Press Start.

4 Lightly oil two baking sheets. Preheat the oven to 200°C/400°F/Gas 6.

5 When the dough cycle has finished, remove the dough from the machine, place it on a lightly floured surface and knock it back (punch it down). Roll it out to a rectangle measuring 23 × 20cm/9 × 8in.

6 Cut into three 20cm/8in long strips. Cut each strip widthways into ten. Roll and stretch each piece to 30cm/12in.

7 Roll in poppy seeds or sea salt if you like. Space well apart on the baking sheets. Brush lightly with olive oil, cover with clear film (plastic wrap) and leave in a warm place for 10–15 minutes.

8 Bake for 15–20 minutes, or until golden, turning once. Transfer to a wire rack to cool.

SOURDOUGHS &
STARTER DOUGH BREADS

*Breads made with starters acquire their wonderful textures and flavours from the multiple
ferments and starter doughs. The bread machine provides the perfect environment to
nurture these doughs. This section also includes a recipe for bread made with fresh yeast.*

RICE BREAD

Rice is an unusual ingredient, but makes delicious bread that is moist, flavoursome and with an interesting texture. The perfect vehicle for leftover cooked rice, it tastes so good that it's worth cooking some specially.

SMALL

180ml/6½fl oz/generous ¾ cup water

1 egg

350g/12oz/3 cups unbleached white bread flour

115g/4oz/1 cup cooked long grain white rice, well drained

15ml/1 tbsp skimmed milk powder

5ml/1 tsp salt

7.5ml/1½ tsp granulated sugar

15g/½oz/1 tbsp butter

5ml/1 tsp easy-blend dried yeast

MEDIUM

240ml/8½fl oz/generous 1 cup water

1 egg

425g/15oz/3¾ cups unbleached white bread flour

150g/5oz/1¼ cups cooked long grain white rice, well drained

22ml/1½ tbsp skimmed milk powder

7.5ml/1½ tsp salt

10ml/2 tsp granulated sugar

15g/½oz/1 tbsp butter

5ml/1 tsp easy-blend dried yeast

LARGE

280ml/10fl oz/1¼ cups water

1 egg

575g/1¼lb/5 cups unbleached white bread flour

200g/7oz/1¾ cups cooked long grain white rice, well drained

30ml/2 tbsp skimmed milk powder

10ml/2 tsp salt

15ml/1 tbsp granulated sugar

20g/¾oz/1½ tbsp butter

10ml/2 tsp easy-blend (rapid-rise) dried yeast

MAKES 1 LOAF

1 Pour the water into the bread machine pan, then add the egg. There is no need to beat the egg before you add it as the machine will mix all of the ingredients together thoroughly. If the instructions for your bread machine specify that the yeast is to be placed in the pan first, simply reverse the order in which you add the liquid and dry ingredients.

2 Sprinkle over the flour, ensuring that it covers the water. Add the rice and milk powder. Add the salt, sugar and butter in separate corners of the bread pan. Make a small indent in the centre of the flour and add the yeast.

3 Set the bread machine to the basic/normal setting, medium crust. Press Start.

4 Remove the bread at the end of the baking cycle and turn out on to a wire rack to cool.

COOK'S TIPS
Make sure the rice is cold before using it in this bread. It is important to drain it very well, or the bread dough may become too moist. Watch the dough as it mixes and add a little more flour if necessary.

SICILIAN SFINCIONE

Sfincione is the Sicilian equivalent of pizza. The Sicilians insist they were making these tasty snacks long before pizzas were made in mainland Italy.

1 Pour the water and oil into the bread pan. If your instructions specify that the yeast is to be placed in the bread pan first, reverse the order in which you add the liquid and the dry ingredients.

2 Sprinkle over the flour, ensuring that it covers the liquid. Add the salt in one corner of the bread pan and the sugar in another corner. Make a small indent in the centre of the flour; add the yeast.

3 Set the bread machine to the dough setting; use basic or pizza dough setting (if available). Press Start. Then lightly oil two baking sheets.

4 Make the topping. Peel and chop the tomatoes. Put in a bowl, add the garlic and 15ml/1 tbsp of the olive oil and toss together. Heat the sunflower oil in a small pan and sauté the onions until softened. Set aside to cool.

5 When the dough cycle has finished, remove the dough from the machine and place it on a lightly floured surface. Knock it back (punch it down) gently and divide it into four equal pieces.

6 Roll each piece of dough out to a round, each about 15–18cm/6–7in in diameter. Space the rounds well apart on the prepared baking sheets, then push up the dough edges on each to make a thin rim. Cover with oiled clear film (plastic wrap) and leave to rise for 10 minutes. Meanwhile, preheat the oven to 220°C/425°F/Gas 7.

7 Sprinkle the topping over the bases, ending with the Pecorino. Season, then drizzle with the remaining olive oil.

8 Bake near the top of the oven for 15–20 minutes or until the base of each sfincione is cooked. Serve immediately.

200ml/7fl oz/⅞cup water
30ml/2 tbsp extra virgin olive oil
350g/12oz/3 cups unbleached white bread flour
7.5ml/1½ tsp salt
2.5ml/½ tsp granulated sugar
5ml/1 tsp easy-blend (rapid-rise) dried yeast

FOR THE TOPPING
6 tomatoes
2 garlic cloves, chopped
45ml/3 tbsp olive oil
15ml/1 tbsp sunflower oil
2 onions, chopped
8 pitted black olives, chopped
10ml/2 tsp dried oregano
90ml/6 tbsp grated Pecorino cheese
salt and freshly ground black pepper

MAKES 4

POTATO BREAD

This golden crusty loaf has a moist soft centre and is perfect for sandwiches.
Use the water in which the potatoes have been cooked to make this bread.
If you haven't got enough, make up the remainder with tap water.

1 Pour the water and sunflower oil into the bread machine pan. However, if the instructions for your machine specify that the yeast is to be placed in the pan first, reverse the order in which you add the liquid and dry ingredients.

2 Sprinkle over the flour, ensuring that it covers the water. Add the mashed potato and milk powder. Add the salt and sugar in separate corners of the bread pan. Make a small indent in the centre of the flour (but not down as far as the liquid) and add the yeast.

3 Set the bread machine to the basic/normal setting, medium crust. Press Start. To glaze the loaf, brush the top with milk either at the beginning of the cooking time or halfway through.

4 Remove the bread at the end of the baking cycle and turn out on to a wire rack to cool.

SMALL
200ml/7fl oz/⅞ cup potato cooking water, at room temperature
30ml/2 tbsp sunflower oil
375g/13oz/3¼ cups unbleached white bread flour
125g/4½oz/1½ cups cold mashed potato
15ml/1 tbsp skimmed milk powder (non fat dry milk)
5ml/1 tsp salt
7.5ml/1½ tsp granulated sugar
5ml/1 tsp easy-blend (rapid-rise) dried yeast
milk, for glazing

MEDIUM
225ml/8fl oz/scant 1 cup potato cooking water, at room temperature
45ml/3 tbsp sunflower oil
500g/1lb 2oz/4½ cups unbleached white bread flour
175g/6oz/2 cups cold mashed potato
22ml/1½ tbsp skimmed milk powder
7.5ml/1½ tsp salt
10ml/2 tsp granulated sugar
7.5ml/1½ tsp easy-blend dried yeast
milk, for glazing

LARGE
330ml/11½fl oz/scant 1½ cups potato cooking water, at room temperature
60ml/4 tbsp sunflower oil
675g/1½lb/6 cups unbleached white bread flour
225g/8oz/2⅔ cups cold cooked mashed potato
30ml/2 tbsp skimmed milk powder
10ml/2 tsp salt
15ml/1 tbsp granulated sugar
7.5ml/1½ tsp easy-blend dried yeast
milk, for glazing

MAKES 1 LOAF

COOK'S TIP
If using leftover potatoes mashed with milk and butter you may need to reduce the liquid a little. If making the mashed potato, use 175g/6oz, 200g/7oz or 275g/10oz raw potatoes, depending on machine size.

PISSALADIÈRE

100ml/3½fl oz/7 tbsp water
1 egg
225g/8oz/2 cups unbleached white
bread flour
5ml/1 tsp salt
25g/1oz/2 tbsp butter
5ml/1 tsp easy-blend (rapid-rise)
dried yeast

FOR THE FILLING
60ml/4 tbsp olive oil
575g/1¼lb onions, thinly sliced
15ml/1 tbsp Dijon mustard
3–4 tomatoes, about 280g/10oz, peeled
and sliced
10ml/2 tsp chopped fresh basil
12 drained canned anchovies
12 black olives
salt and freshly ground black pepper

SERVES 6

This French version of an Italian pizza is typical of Niçoise dishes, with anchovies and olives providing the distinctive flavour typical of the region.

1 Pour the water and egg into the machine pan. If the instructions for your machine specify that the yeast is to be added first, reverse the order in which you add the liquid and the dry ingredients.

2 Sprinkle over the white bread flour, ensuring that it completely covers the water and the egg. Add the salt in one corner of the pan and the butter in another corner. Make a small indent in the centre of the flour (but not down as far as the liquid) and add the easy-blend dried yeast.

3 Set the bread machine to the dough setting; use basic or pizza dough setting (if available). Press Start. Then lightly oil a 27 × 20cm/11 × 8in Swiss (jelly) roll tin (pan) that is about 1cm/½in deep.

4 Make the filling. Heat the olive oil in a large frying pan and cook the onions over a low heat for about 20 minutes, until very soft. Set aside to cool.

5 When the dough cycle has finished, remove the dough from the machine and place it on a lightly floured surface. Knock it back (punch it down) gently, then roll it out to a rectangle measuring about 30 × 23cm/12 × 9in. Place in the prepared tin, and press outwards and upwards, so that the dough covers the base and sides.

6 Spread the mustard over the dough. Arrange the tomato slices on top. Season the onions with salt, pepper and basil and spread the mixture over the tomatoes.

7 Arrange the anchovies in a lattice and dot with the olives. Cover with oiled clear film (plastic wrap) and leave to rise for 10–15 minutes. Meanwhile preheat the oven to 200°C/400°F/Gas 6. Bake the pissaladière for 25–30 minutes, or until the base is cooked and golden around the edges. Serve hot or warm.

SPECIALITY GRAINS

This selection of recipes includes classic flours from around the world, producing loaves with a variety of textures and flavours. Gluten is an essential part of the structure of bread, to ensure an open, light crumb and texture. Most grains other than wheat have little or no gluten, so millet, buckwheat, oats and rye have been blended with wheat flours to provide rich, nutty flavoured loaves which can be successfully baked in your bread machine.

ONION FOCACCIA

Focaccia, with its characteristic texture and dimpled surface, has become hugely popular in recent years. This version has a delectable red onion and fresh sage topping.

210ml/7½fl oz/scant 1 cup water
15ml/1 tbsp olive oil
350g/12oz/3 cups unbleached white bread flour
2.5ml/½ tsp salt
5ml/1 tsp granulated sugar
5ml/1 tsp easy-blend (rapid-rise) dried yeast
15ml/1 tbsp chopped fresh sage
15ml/1 tbsp chopped red onion

FOR THE TOPPING
30ml/2 tbsp olive oil
½ red onion, thinly sliced
5 fresh sage leaves
10ml/2 tsp coarse sea salt
coarsely ground black pepper

MAKES 1 FOCACCIA

1 Pour the water and oil into the bread pan. Reverse the order in which you add the wet and dry ingredients if necessary.

2 Sprinkle over the flour, ensuring that it covers the liquid. Add the salt and sugar in separate corners. Make a small indent in the flour and add the yeast.

3 Set the bread machine to the dough setting. If your machine has a choice of settings use the basic or pizza dough setting. Press Start.

4 Lightly oil a 25–28cm/10–11in shallow round cake tin or pizza pan. When the cycle has finished, remove the dough from the pan and place it on a surface lightly dusted with flour.

5 Knock the dough back (punch it down) and flatten it slightly. Sprinkle over the sage and red onion and knead gently to incorporate. Shape the dough into a ball, flatten it, then roll it into a round of about 25–28cm/10–11in. Place in the prepared tin. Cover with oiled clear film (plastic wrap) and leave to rise in a warm place for 20 minutes.

6 Meanwhile, preheat the oven to 200°C/400°F/Gas 6. Uncover the risen focaccia, and, using your fingertips, poke the dough to make deep dimples over the surface. Cover and leave to rise for 10–15 minutes, or until the dough has doubled in bulk.

7 Drizzle over the olive oil and sprinkle with the onion, sage leaves, sea salt and black pepper. Bake for 20–25 minutes, or until golden. Turn out on to a wire rack to cool slightly. Serve warm.

BRAN AND YOGURT BREAD

This soft-textured yogurt bread is enriched with bran. It is high in fibre and makes wonderful toast.

SMALL

150ml/5fl oz/⅔ cup water
125ml/4½fl oz/generous ½ cup natural (plain) yogurt
15ml/1 tbsp sunflower oil
15ml/1 tbsp molasses
200g/7oz/1¾ cups unbleached white bread flour
150g/5½oz/1⅓ cups wholemeal (whole-wheat) bread flour
25g/1oz/⅓ cup wheat bran
5ml/1 tsp salt
4ml/¾ tsp easy-blend (rapid-rise) dried yeast

MEDIUM

185ml/6½fl oz/generous ¾ cup water
175ml/6fl oz/¾ cup natural yogurt
22ml/1½ tbsp sunflower oil
30ml/2 tbsp molasses
260g/generous 9oz/2⅓ cups unbleached white bread flour
200g/7oz/1¾ cups wholemeal bread flour
40g/1½oz/½ cup wheat bran
7.5ml/1½ tsp salt
5ml/1 tsp easy-blend dried yeast

LARGE

230ml/8fl oz/1 cup water
210ml/7½fl oz/scant 1 cup natural yogurt
30ml/2 tbsp sunflower oil
30ml/2 tbsp molasses
375g/13oz/3¼ cups unbleached white bread flour
250g/9oz/2¼ cups wholemeal bread flour
50g/2oz/⅔ cup wheat bran
10ml/2 tsp salt
7.5ml/1½ tsp easy-blend dried yeast

MAKES 1 LOAF

COOK'S TIP
Molasses is added to this bread to give added flavour and colour. You can use treacle or golden (light corn) syrup instead, to intensify or lessen the flavour respectively, if desired.

1 Pour the water, yogurt, oil and molasses into the bread machine pan. If the instructions for your machine specify that the yeast is to be placed in the pan first, reverse the order in which you add the liquid and dry ingredients.

2 Sprinkle over both the white and the wholemeal flours, ensuring that the liquid mixture is completely covered. Add the wheat bran and salt, then make a small indent in the centre of the dry ingredients (but not down as far as the liquid) and add the easy-blend dried yeast.

3 Set the bread machine to the basic/normal setting, medium crust. Press Start.

4 Remove the bread from the pan at the end of the baking cycle and turn out on to a wire rack to cool. Serve when still just warm, if you like.

Speciality Grains

OLIVE FOUGASSE

210ml/7½fl oz/scant 1 cup water
15ml/1 tbsp olive oil, plus extra
for brushing
350g/12oz/3 cups unbleached white
bread flour
5ml/1 tsp salt
5ml/1 tsp granulated sugar
5ml/1 tsp easy-blend (rapid-rise)
dried yeast
50g/2oz/½ cup pitted black
olives, chopped

MAKES 1 FOUGASSE

A French hearth bread, fougasse is traditionally baked on the floor of the hot bread oven, just after the fire has been raked out. It can be left plain or flavoured with olives, herbs, nuts or cheese.

1 Pour the water and the oil into the machine pan. Reverse the order in which you add wet and dry ingredients if necessary. Sprinkle over the flour, ensuring that it covers the liquid. Add the salt in one corner of the bread pan and the sugar in another corner. Make a small indent in the centre of the flour (but not down as far as the liquid) and add the yeast.

2 Set the bread machine to the dough setting; use basic or pizza dough setting (if available). Press Start. When the cycle has finished, remove the dough from the machine and place it on a lightly floured surface.

3 Knock the dough back (punch it down) gently and flatten it slightly. Sprinkle over the olives and fold over the dough two or three times to incorporate them.

4 Flatten the dough and roll it into an oblong, about 30cm/12in long. With a sharp knife make four or five parallel cuts diagonally through the body of the dough, but leaving the edges intact. Gently stretch the fougasse dough so that it resembles a ladder.

5 Lightly oil a baking sheet, then place the shaped dough on it. Cover with oiled clear film (plastic wrap) and leave in a warm place for about 30 minutes, or until the dough has doubled in bulk.

6 Preheat the oven to 220°C/425°F/ Gas 7. Brush the top of the fougasse with olive oil, place in the oven and bake about for 20–25 minutes, or until the bread is golden. Turn out on to a wire rack to cool.

POLENTA AND WHOLEMEAL LOAF

Polenta adds an interesting grainy quality to the texture of this rich wholemeal bread, which is perfect for everyday use.

SMALL
220ml/scant 8fl oz/scant 1 cup water
30ml/2 tbsp clear honey
25g/1oz/2 tbsp polenta
25g/1oz/¼ cup unbleached white
bread flour
325g/11½oz/scant 3 cups wholemeal
(whole-wheat) bread flour
5ml/1 tsp salt
20g/¾oz/1½ tbsp butter
4ml/¾ tsp easy-blend (rapid-rise)
dried yeast

MEDIUM
300ml/10½fl oz/1¼ cups water
45ml/3 tbsp clear honey
50g/2oz/scant ½ cup polenta
50g/2oz/½ cup unbleached white
bread flour
400g/14oz/3½ cups wholemeal
bread flour
7.5ml/1½ tsp salt
25g/1oz/2 tbsp butter
7.5ml/1½ tsp easy-blend dried yeast

LARGE
350ml/12fl oz/1½ cups water
60ml/4 tbsp clear honey
75g/3oz/scant ¾ cup polenta
75g/3oz/¾ cup unbleached white
bread flour
525g/1lb 3oz/4¾ cups wholemeal
bread flour
10ml/2 tsp salt
40g/1½oz/3 tbsp butter
10ml/2 tsp easy-blend dried yeast

MAKES 1 LOAF

1 Add the water and honey to the pan. If necessary, reverse the order in which you add the liquid and dry ingredients. Sprinkle over the polenta and flours, ensuring that the liquid is covered.

2 Add the salt and butter in separate corners of the pan. Make a small indent in the centre of the flour (but not down as far as the liquid) and add the yeast.

3 Set the machine to the whole wheat setting, medium crust. Press Start.

COOK'S TIP
This bread is perfect for breakfast and it may be baked using the automatic delay timer. The small quantity of butter should be fine overnight, but if you wish, substitute vegetable oil and adjust the liquid accordingly.

4 Remove the loaf from the bread pan at the end of the baking cycle and turn out on to a wire rack to cool.

CARTA DI MUSICA

This crunchy, crisp bread looks like sheets of music manuscript paper, which is how it came by its name. It originated in Sardinia and can be found throughout southern Italy, where it is eaten not only as a bread, but as a substitute for pasta in lasagne. It also makes a good pizza base.

280ml/10fl oz/1¼ cups water
450g/1lb/4 cups unbleached white bread flour
7.5ml/1½ tsp salt
5ml/1 tsp granulated sugar
5ml/1 tsp easy-blend (rapid-rise) dried yeast

MAKES 8

COOK'S TIP
Cutting the partially cooked breads in half is quite tricky. You may find it easier to divide the dough into six or eight pieces, and roll these as thinly as possible before baking. The cutting stage can then be avoided.

5 Now roll out the other three pieces. If the dough starts to tear, cover it with oiled clear film (plastic wrap)and leave it to rest for 2–3 minutes.

6 When all the dough has been rolled out, cover with oiled clear film and leave to rest on the floured surface for 10–15 minutes. Preheat the oven to 230°C/450°F/Gas 8. Place two baking sheets in the oven to heat.

1 Pour the water into the bread machine pan. If the instructions specify that the yeast should be placed in the pan first, simply reverse the order in which you add the liquid and dry ingredients to the pan.

2 Sprinkle over the white bread flour, ensuring that it covers the water. Add the salt in one corner of the bread pan and the sugar in another corner. Make a small indent in the centre of the flour (but not down as far as the liquid) and add the easy-blend dried yeast.

3 Set the bread machine to the dough setting; use basic dough setting (if available). Press Start.

4 When the dough cycle has finished, remove the dough from the machine and place it on a lightly floured surface. Knock it back (punch it down) gently and divide it into four equal pieces. Shape each piece of dough into a ball, then roll a piece out until about 3mm/⅛in thick.

7 Keeping the other dough rounds covered, place one round on each baking sheet. Bake for 5 minutes, or until puffed up.

8 Remove from the oven and cut each round in half horizontally to make two thinner breads. Place these cut side up on the baking sheets, return them to the oven and bake for 5–8 minutes more, until crisp. Turn out on to a wire rack and cook the remaining breads.

TOASTED MILLET AND RYE BREAD

300ml/10½fl oz/1¼ cups water
50g/2oz/½ cup rye flour
*450g/1lb/4 cups unbleached white
bread flour*
25g/1oz/¼ cup millet flakes
*15ml/1 tbsp light muscovado
(brown) sugar*
5ml/1 tsp salt
25g/1oz/2 tbsp butter
*5ml/1 tsp easy-blend (rapid-rise)
dried yeast*
50g/2oz/⅓ cup millet seeds
millet flour, for dusting
MAKES 1 LOAF

COOK'S TIP
Before adding, toast the millet seeds
under a preheated grill (broiler) to
enhance their distinctive sweet flavour.

*The dough for this delectable loaf is made in the bread machine, but it is
shaped by hand before being baked in the oven.*

1 Pour the water into the bread pan. If
the instructions for your bread machine
specify that the yeast is to be placed in
the pan first, reverse the order in which
you add the liquid and dry ingredients.

2 Sprinkle over both types of flour, then
add the millet flakes, ensuring that the
water is completely covered. Add the
sugar, salt and butter, placing them in
separate corners. Make an indent in the
centre of the flour (but not down as far
as the liquid) and add the yeast.

3 Set the bread machine to the dough
setting; use basic raisin dough setting
(if available). Press Start. Add the millet
seeds when the machine beeps or
during the last 5 minutes of kneading.
Lightly flour a baking sheet.

4 When the dough cycle has finished,
knock the dough back (punch it down)
gently on a lightly floured surface.

5 Shape the dough into a rectangle. Roll it
up lengthways, then shape it into a thick
baton with square ends. Place it on the
prepared baking sheet, making sure that the
seam is underneath. Cover it with lightly oiled
clear film (plastic wrap) and leave in a warm
place for 30–45 minutes, or until almost
doubled in size.

6 Remove the clear film and dust the
top of the loaf with the millet flour.
Using a sharp knife, make slanting cuts
in alternate directions along the top of
the loaf. Leave it to stand for about
10 minutes. Meanwhile, preheat the
oven to 220°C/425°F/Gas 7.

7 Bake the loaf for 25–30 minutes, or
until golden and hollow-sounding. Turn
out on to a wire rack to cool.

GARLIC AND CORIANDER NAAN

100ml/3½ fl oz/7 tbsp water
60ml/4 tbsp natural (plain) yogurt
280g/10oz/2½ cups unbleached white
bread flour
1 garlic clove, finely chopped
5ml/1 tsp black onion seeds
5ml/1 tsp ground coriander
5ml/1 tsp salt
10ml/2 tsp clear honey
15ml/1 tbsp melted ghee or butter,
plus 30–45ml/2–3 tbsp
5ml/1 tsp easy-blend (rapid-rise)
dried yeast
15ml/1 tbsp chopped fresh
coriander (cilantro)

MAKES 3

VARIATION

For a basic naan omit the coriander,
garlic and black onion seeds. Include
a little ground black pepper or chilli
powder for a slightly piquant note.

Indian restaurants the world over have introduced us to several differently flavoured examples of this leavened flatbread, and this version is particularly tasty and will become a great favourite. The bread is traditionally made in a tandoor oven, but this method has been developed to give almost identical results.

1 Pour the water and natural yogurt into the bread machine pan. If the instructions for your bread machine specify that the easy-blend dried yeast is to be placed in the pan first, then simply reverse the order in which you add the liquid and dry ingredients.

2 Sprinkle over the flour, ensuring that it covers the liquid completely. Add the garlic, black onion seeds and ground coriander. Add the salt, honey and the 15ml/1 tbsp melted ghee or butter in separate corners of the bread pan. Make a small indent in the centre of the flour (but not down as far as the liquid) and add the easy-blend dried yeast.

3 Set the bread machine to the dough setting; use basic or pizza dough setting (if available). Press Start.

4 When the dough cycle has finished, preheat the oven to its highest setting. Place three baking sheets in the oven to heat. Remove the dough from the breadmaking machine and place it on a lightly floured surface.

5 Knock the naan dough back (punch it down) gently and then knead in the chopped fresh coriander. Divide the dough into three equal pieces.

6 Shape each piece into a ball and cover two of the pieces with oiled clear film (plastic wrap). Roll out the remaining piece of dough into a large teardrop shape, making it about 5–8mm/¼–⅓in thick. Cover with oiled clear film while you roll out the remaining two pieces of dough to make two more naan.

7 Preheat the grill (broiler) to its highest setting. Place the naan on the preheated baking sheets and then bake them for 4–5 minutes, until puffed up. Remove the baking sheets from the oven and place them under the hot grill for a few seconds, until the naan start to brown and blister.

8 Brush the naan with melted ghee or butter and serve warm.

Flatbreads & Pizzas

BUCKWHEAT AND WALNUT BREAD

Buckwheat flour is made from toasted buckwheat groats. It has a distinctive earthy taste, perfectly mellowed when blended with white flour and walnuts in this compact bread, flavoured with molasses.

SMALL
210ml/7½fl oz/scant 1 cup water
10ml/2 tsp molasses
22ml/1½ tbsp walnut or olive oil
315g/11oz/2¾ cups unbleached white
bread flour
50g/2oz/½ cup buckwheat flour
15ml/1 tbsp skimmed milk powder
(non fat dry milk)
5ml/1 tsp salt
2.5ml/½ tsp granulated sugar
5ml/1 tsp easy-blend (rapid-rise)
dried yeast
40g/1½oz/⅓ cup walnut pieces

MEDIUM
15ml/3 tsp molasses
315ml/11fl oz/1⅓ cups water
30ml/2 tbsp walnut or olive oil
425g/15oz/3¾ cups unbleached white
bread flour
75g/3oz/¾ cup buckwheat flour
22ml/1½ tbsp skimmed milk powder
7.5ml/1½ tsp salt
4ml/¾ tsp granulated sugar
5ml/1 tsp easy-blend dried yeast
50g/2oz/½ cup walnut pieces

LARGE
420ml/15fl oz/generous 1¾ cups water
20ml/4 tsp molasses
45ml/3 tbsp walnut or olive oil
575g/1¼lb/5 cups unbleached white
bread flour
115g/4oz/1 cup buckwheat flour
30ml/2 tbsp skimmed milk powder
10ml/2 tsp salt
5ml/1 tsp granulated sugar
7.5ml/1½ tsp easy-blend dried yeast
75g/3oz/¾ cup walnut pieces

MAKES 1 LOAF

1 Pour the water, molasses and walnut or olive oil into the bread pan. If the instructions for your machine specify that the yeast is to be placed in the pan first, reverse the order in which you add the liquid and dry ingredients.

2 Sprinkle over the flours, covering the liquid. Add the milk powder. Place the salt and sugar in separate corners. Make a small indent in the centre of the flour (but not down as far as the liquid) and add the easy-blend dried yeast.

3 Set the bread machine to the basic/normal setting; use raisin setting (if available), medium crust. Press Start. Add the walnut pieces when the machine beeps or after the first kneading.

4 Remove the bread from the machine pan at the end of the baking cycle and turn out on to a wire rack.

FLATBREADS & PIZZAS

Flatbreads are fun to bake and make delicious meal accompaniments. Naan, often flavoured with coriander or black onion seeds, is typical of Indian flatbread, and Fougasse is a traditional French hearth bread. Italy is famous for Focaccia, pizzas and Carta di Musica, while the French version of pizza is the Pissaladière. All of these breads can be made in your machine using the "dough only" setting and then hand-shaped and oven-baked.

FOUR SEED BREAD

This light wholemeal and millet bread has added bite, thanks to a variety of tasty seeds, all readily available from your local health-food store.

280ml/10fl oz/1¼ cups water
30ml/2 tbsp extra virgin olive oil
400g/14oz/3½ cups unbleached white bread flour
50g/2oz/½ cup millet flour
50g/2oz/½ cup wholemeal (whole-wheat) bread flour
15ml/1 tbsp granulated sugar
10ml/2 tsp salt
5ml/1 tsp easy-blend (rapid rise) dried yeast
30ml/2 tbsp pumpkin seeds
30ml/2 tbsp sunflower seeds
22ml/1½ tbsp linseeds
22ml/1½ tbsp sesame seeds, lightly toasted
15ml/1 tbsp milk
30ml/2 tbsp golden linseeds

MAKES 1 LOAF

1 Pour the water and oil into the bread pan. Reverse the order in which you add the wet and dry ingredients if your machine specifies this.

2 Sprinkle over all three types of flour, ensuring that the water is completely covered. Add the sugar and salt in separate corners of the bread pan.

3 Make a shallow indent in the centre of the flour and add the yeast. Set the bread machine to the dough setting; use basic raisin dough setting (if available). Press Start. Add the seeds when the machine beeps to add extra ingredients or during the last 5 minutes of kneading.

4 When the dough cycle has finished, place the dough on a lightly floured surface and knock back (punch down) gently.

5 Lightly oil a baking sheet. Shape the dough into a round flat loaf. Make a hole in the centre with your finger. Gradually enlarge the cavity, turning the dough, until you have a ring. Place the ring on the baking sheet. Cover it with lightly oiled clear film (plastic wrap) and leave in a warm place for 30–45 minutes, or until the dough has doubled in size.

6 Meanwhile, preheat the oven to 200°C/400°F/Gas 6. Brush the top of the bread with milk and sprinkle it with the golden linseeds. Make slashes around the loaf, radiating outwards.

7 Bake for 30–35 minutes, or until golden and hollow-sounding. Turn out on to a wire rack to cool.

MAPLE AND OATMEAL LOAF

Rolled oats and oat bran add texture to this wholesome bread, which is suffused with the delectable flavour of maple syrup.

1 Pour the water into the bread machine pan and then add the maple syrup. If the instructions for your machine specify that the yeast is to be placed in the pan first, reverse the order in which you add the liquid and dry ingredients.

2 Sprinkle over both the white and wholemeal flours, then the rolled oats and oat bran, ensuring that the water is completely covered.

3 Add the salt, sugar and butter, placing them in separate corners of the bread pan. Make a small indent in the centre of the flour (but not down as far as the liquid) and add the yeast.

4 Set the bread machine to the basic/normal setting, medium crust. Press Start.

5 Remove the bread at the end of the baking cycle and turn out on to a wire rack to cool.

SMALL
210ml/7½fl oz/scant 1 cup water
15ml/1 tbsp maple syrup
300g/11oz/3⅔ cups unbleached white bread flour
50g/2oz/½ cup wholemeal (whole-wheat) bread flour
20g/⅔oz/¼ cup rolled oats
15ml/1 tbsp oat bran
5ml/1 tsp salt
5ml/1 tsp granulated sugar
25g/1oz/2 tbsp butter
5ml/1 tsp easy-blend (rapid-rise) dried yeast

MEDIUM
315ml/11fl oz/1⅓ cups water
30ml/2 tbsp maple syrup
375g/13oz/3¼ cups unbleached white bread flour
75g/3oz/¾ cup wholemeal bread flour
40g/1½oz/½ cup rolled oats
30ml/2 tbsp oat bran
5ml/1 tsp salt
5ml/1 tsp granulated sugar
40g/1½oz/3 tbsp butter
5ml/1 tsp easy-blend dried yeast

LARGE
410ml/14½fl oz/1¾ cups water
45ml/3 tbsp maple syrup
500g/1lb 2oz/4½ cups unbleached white bread flour
115g/4oz/1 cup wholemeal bread flour
50g/2oz/⅔ cup rolled oats
45ml/3 tbsp oat bran
7.5ml/1½ tsp salt
7.5ml/1½ tsp granulated sugar
50g/2oz/¼ cup butter
7.5ml/1½ tsp easy-blend dried yeast

MAKES 1 LOAF

COOK'S TIP
Use 100 per cent pure maple syrup. Less expensive products are often blended with cane or corn syrup, which does not have the smooth rich flavour of the real thing.

HAZELNUT AND FIG BREAD

This healthy, high-fibre bread is flavoured with figs and hazelnuts.

1 Pour the water and the lemon juice into the bread machine pan. If the instructions for your machine specify that the yeast is to be placed in the pan first, reverse the order in which you add the liquid and dry ingredients.

2 Sprinkle over the flours, then the wheatgerm, covering the water. Add the milk powder. Add the salt, sugar and butter in separate corners. Make an indent in the flour; add the yeast.

3 Set the bread machine to the basic/normal setting; use raisin setting (if available), medium crust. Press Start. Coarsely chop the dried figs. Add the hazelnuts and the figs to the bread pan when the machine beeps or after the first kneading has finished.

4 Remove the bread at the end of the baking cycle and turn out on to a wire rack to allow to cool.

SMALL
230ml/8fl oz/1 cup water
5ml/1 tsp lemon juice
280g/10oz/2½ cups unbleached white
bread flour
75g/3oz/¾ cup brown bread flour
45ml/3 tbsp toasted wheatgerm
15ml/1 tbsp skimmed milk powder
(non fat dry milk)
5ml/1 tsp salt
10ml/2 tsp granulated sugar
20g/¾oz/1½ tbsp butter
5ml/1 tsp easy-blend (rapid-rise)
dried yeast
25g/1oz/3 tbsp ready-to-eat dried figs
25g/1oz/3 tbsp skinned hazelnuts,
roasted and chopped

MEDIUM
280ml/10fl oz/1¼ cups water
7.5ml/1½ tsp lemon juice
350g/12oz/3 cups unbleached white
bread flour
100g/3½oz/scant 1 cup brown
bread flour
60ml/4 tbsp toasted wheatgerm
30ml/2 tbsp skimmed milk powder
7.5ml/1½ tsp salt
15ml/1 tbsp granulated sugar
25g/1oz/2 tbsp butter
7.5ml/1½ tsp easy-blend dried yeast
40g/1½oz/¼ cup ready-to-eat dried figs
40g/1½oz/⅓ cup skinned hazelnuts,
roasted and chopped

LARGE
450ml/16fl oz/scant 2 cups water
10ml/2 tsp lemon juice
500g/1lb 2oz/4½ cups unbleached
white bread flour
115g/4oz/1 cup brown bread flour
75ml/5 tbsp toasted wheatgerm
45ml/3 tbsp skimmed milk powder
10ml/2 tsp salt
20ml/4 tsp granulated sugar
40g/1½oz/3 tbsp butter
7.5ml/1½ tsp easy-blend dried yeast
50g/2oz/⅓ cup ready-to-eat dried figs
50g/2oz/½ cup skinned hazelnuts,
roasted and chopped

MAKES 1 LOAF

RUSSIAN BLACK BREAD

SMALL

230ml/8fl oz/1 cup water
30ml/2 tbsp sunflower oil
30ml/2 tbsp molasses
115g/4oz/1 cup rye flour
*50g/2oz/½ cup wholemeal
(whole-wheat) bread flour*
*175g/6oz/1½ cups unbleached white
bread flour*
25g/1oz/2 tbsp oat bran
50g/2oz/½ cup dried breadcrumbs
15ml/1 tbsp cocoa powder (unsweetened)
30ml/2 tbsp instant coffee granules
7.5ml/1½ tsp caraway seeds
5ml/1 tsp salt
*5ml/1 tsp easy-blend (rapid-rise)
dried yeast*

MEDIUM

360ml/12½fl oz/generous 1½ cups water
30ml/2 tbsp sunflower oil
40ml/2½ tbsp molasses
140g/5oz/1¼ cups rye flour
85g/3oz/¾ cup wholemeal bread flour
*250g/9oz/2¼ cups unbleached white
bread flour*
40g/1½oz/3 tbsp oat bran
75g/3oz/¾ cup dried breadcrumbs
22ml/1½ tbsp cocoa powder
40ml/2½ tbsp instant coffee granules
7.5ml/1½ tsp caraway seeds
7.5ml/1½ tsp salt
7.5ml/1½ tsp easy-blend dried yeast

LARGE

430ml/15fl oz/generous 1⅔ cups water
45ml/3 tbsp sunflower oil
45ml/3 tbsp molasses
200g/7oz/1¾ cups rye flour
*100g/3½oz/scant 1 cup wholemeal
bread flour*
*300g/10½oz/generous 2½ cups
unbleached white bread flour*
50g/2oz/4 tbsp oat bran
100g/3½oz/scant 1 cup dried breadcrumbs
30ml/2 tbsp cocoa powder
45ml/3 tbsp instant coffee granules
10ml/2 tsp caraway seeds
10ml/2 tsp salt
10ml/2 tsp easy-blend dried yeast

MAKES 1 LOAF

European rye breads often include cocoa and coffee to add colour to this dark traditionally dense, chewy bread. Slice it thinly, serve it with cold meats or pâtés or use it as the basis of an open sandwich.

1 Pour the water, sunflower oil and molasses into the bread machine pan. If the instructions for your machine specify that the yeast is to be placed in the bread pan first, then simply reverse the order in which you add the liquid and dry ingredients.

2 Sprinkle over the rye, wholemeal and white flours, then the oat bran and breadcrumbs, ensuring that the water is completely covered. Add the cocoa powder, coffee granules, caraway seeds and salt. Make a small indent in the centre of the flour (but not down as far as the liquid) and add the easy-blend dried yeast.

3 Set the bread machine to the whole wheat setting, medium crust and then press Start.

4 Remove the bread at the end of the baking cycle and turn out on to a wire rack to cool.

SPELT AND BULGUR WHEAT BREAD

Two unusual grains are used here. Spelt is a variety of wheat which is not widely grown, but is ground by some specialist millers. Cracked wheat or bulgur is the cracked wheat berry which has been softened by steaming. It contributes crunch while the spelt flour adds a nutty flavour.

SMALL
110ml/scant 4fl oz/scant ½ cup water
100ml/3½fl oz/7 tbsp buttermilk
5ml/1 tsp lemon juice
250g/9oz/2¼ cups unbleached white bread flour
100g/3½oz/scant 1 cup spelt flour
30ml/2 tbsp bulgur wheat
5ml/1 tsp salt
10ml/2 tsp granulated sugar
5ml/1 tsp easy-blend (rapid-rise) dried yeast

MEDIUM
220ml/scant 8fl oz/scant 1 cup water
125ml/4½fl oz/generous ½ cup buttermilk
7.5ml/1½ tsp lemon juice
350g/12oz/3 cups unbleached white bread flour
150g/5½oz/1⅓ cups spelt flour
45ml/3 tbsp bulgur wheat
7.5ml/1½ tsp salt
15ml/1 tbsp granulated sugar
7.5ml/1½ tsp easy-blend dried yeast

LARGE
280ml/10fl oz/1¼ cups water
140ml/5fl oz/⅝ cup buttermilk
10ml/2 tsp lemon juice
425g/15oz/3¾ cups unbleached white bread flour
200g/7oz/1¾ cups spelt flour
60ml/4 tbsp bulgur wheat
10ml/2 tsp salt
20ml/4 tsp granulated sugar
10ml/2 tsp easy-blend dried yeast

MAKES 1 LOAF

VARIATION
The buttermilk adds a characteristic slightly sour note to this bread. You can replace it with low-fat natural (plain) yogurt or semi-skimmed (low-fat) milk for a less tangy flavour.

1 Pour the water, buttermilk and lemon juice into the bread machine pan. If the instructions for your machine specify that the yeast is to be placed in the pan first, reverse the order in which you add the liquid and dry ingredients.

2 Sprinkle over both types of flour, then the bulgur wheat, ensuring that the liquid is completely covered. Add the salt and sugar, placing them in separate corners of the bread pan.

3 Make a small indent in the centre of the flour (but not down as far as the liquid) and add the yeast.

4 Set the bread machine to the basic/normal setting, medium crust. Press Start.

5 Remove the bread at the end of the baking cycle and turn out on to a wire rack to allow to cool.

MULTIGRAIN BREAD

This healthy, mixed grain bread owes its wonderfully rich flavour to honey and malt extract.

1 Add the water, honey and malt extract to the pan. If your machine's instructions specify that the yeast is to be placed in the pan first, reverse the order in which you add the liquid and dry ingredients.

2 Sprinkle over all four types of flour, ensuring that the liquid is completely covered. Add the jumbo oats and skimmed milk powder.

3 Place the salt and butter in separate corners of the bread machine pan. Make a small indent in the centre of the flour (but not down as far as the liquid) and add the yeast.

4 Set the bread machine to the whole wheat setting, medium crust. Press Start. Remove the bread at the end of the baking cycle and turn out on to a wire rack to allow to cool.

SMALL
230ml/8fl oz/1 cup water
15ml/1 tbsp clear honey
7.5ml/1½ tsp malt extract
115g/4oz/1 cup Granary
(whole-wheat) flour
50g/2oz/½ cup rye flour
75g/3oz/¾ cup unbleached white
bread flour
140g/5oz/1¼ cups wholemeal
(whole-wheat) bread flour
15ml/1 tbsp jumbo oats
15ml/1 tbsp skimmed milk powder
(non fat dry milk)
5ml/1 tsp salt
20g/¾oz/1½ tbsp butter
4ml/¾ tsp easy-blend (rapid-rise)
dried yeast

MEDIUM
300ml/10½fl oz/scant 1⅓ cups water
30ml/2 tbsp clear honey
15ml/1 tbsp malt extract
150g/5½oz/1⅓ cups Granary flour
75g/3oz/¾ cup rye flour
75g/3oz/¾ cup unbleached white
bread flour
200g/7oz/1¾ cups wholemeal
bread flour
30ml/2 tbsp jumbo oats
30ml/2 tbsp skimmed milk powder
7.5ml/1½ tsp salt
25g/1oz/2 tbsp butter
5ml/1 tsp easy-blend dried yeast

LARGE
375ml/13fl oz/scant 1⅔ cups water
30ml/2 tbsp clear honey
22ml/1½ tbsp malt extract
200g/7oz/1¾cups Granary flour
115g/4oz/1 cup rye flour
115g/4oz/1 cup unbleached white
bread flour
225g/8oz/2 cups wholemeal
bread flour
45ml/3 tbsp jumbo oats
45ml/3 tbsp skimmed milk powder
10ml/2 tsp salt
40g/1½ oz/3 tbsp butter
7.5ml/1½ tsp easy-blend dried yeast

MAKES 1 LOAF